# HOW TO U

The contents page of this book shows ho
book is in two main sections: general inf
tourist regions with an introduction and
of Lisbon (detail below right). All main e
maps. Places to visit and leisure facilities
symbols. Main roads, railw

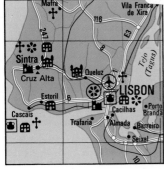

**Regional Maps**

**Town Plan**

| | | | | |
|---|---|---|---|---|
| 🖼 | Museum/gallery | | 🌲 | Pine Woods |
| ✝ | Religious building | | 🏰 | Palace |
| ✈ | Main airport | | | |
| ✈ | Local airport | | | |
| 🏰 | Castle | | | |
| 🏛 | Interesting building | | | |
| ɱ | Ancient site/monument | | | |
| ❀ | Gardens | | | |
| ● | Park | | | |
| ⋔ | Spa | | | |
| ϴ | Caves | | | |
| ◗ | Walking/hiking | | | |
| ⚡ | Winter sports | | | |
| 🌲 | National park | | | |

*PORTUGAL*

| metres | feet |
|---|---|
| 1500 | 4921 |
| 1000 | 3281 |
| 400 | 1312 |
| 200 | 656 |
| 0 | 0 |

| | |
|---|---|
| 🖼 | Museum/gallery |
| ✝ | Religious building |
| 🏰 | Castle |
| 🏛 | Interesting building |
| ▣ | Theatre |
| 📖 | Library |
| ✗ | City hall |
| ✉ | Post office |
| ℹ | Information |
| ● | Park |
| ❀ | Garden |
| ● | Railway station |
| ⬛ | Bus terminal |
| Ⓟ | Car park |
| ⊕ | Hospital |

| | |
|---|---|
| ═══ | motorway |
| ╌╌╌ | motorway under construction |
| ─── | other roads |
| ─── | railway |

Every effort has been made to give you an up-to-date text but changes are constantly occurring and we will be grateful for any information about changes you may notice while you are travelling.

# CONTENTS

# PORTUGAL

Welcome to Portugal
R.A.N. Dixon

Collins
Glasgow and London

**Cover Photographs**

top: Local costume, Minho; Portuguese National Tourist Office
Middle left: Monument to Navigators, Lisbon; Feature-Pix
Middle right: Fisherman's Beach, Albufeira; Van Phillips
Sunflowers in Alentejo; Feature-Pix   Boys on a donkey; Van Phillips

**Photographs**

Van Phillips
pp. 9, 35, 42, 44, 45 (bottom), 47 (top right; middle), 48, 53 (top), 55, 73, 78, 79, 80–81, 84, 87, 88–89, 91

Portuguese National Tourist Office
pp. 21, 25, 31 (left), 34 (bottom right), 38, 40 (bottom), 47–48 (bottom), 49 (bottom), 64 (top), 66, 67 (bottom), 71 (bottom), 76 (left), 86 (bottom

J. Allan Cash
pp. 30, 34 (top), 40 (top), 46, 53 (bottom), 56, 58, 62–63, 70 (bottom), 71 (top), 72, 77

Picturepoint
pp. 27, 29 (top), 31 (right), 34 (middle), 37, 39 (bottom), 65, 67 (top), 70 (top), 82

Photobank
pp. 39 (top), 41, 45 (top), 47 (top left), 54, 75, 83, 85, 86 (top), 90

Feature-Pix
pp. 29 (bottom), 42 (inset), 57

ZEFA
pp. 49 (top), 52, 64 (bottom)

**Regional Maps**
Mike Shand, Kažia L. Kram, Iaxin Gerard

**Town Plan**
M. & R. Piggott

**Illustrations**
pp. 6–7 Peter Joyce
p. 14 Barry Rowe

First published 1984
Copyright © text: R.A.N. Dixon 1984
Copyright © maps: Wm. Collins Sons & Co. Ltd.
Published by William Collins Sons and Company Limited
Printed in Great Britain
ISBN 0 00 447332 9

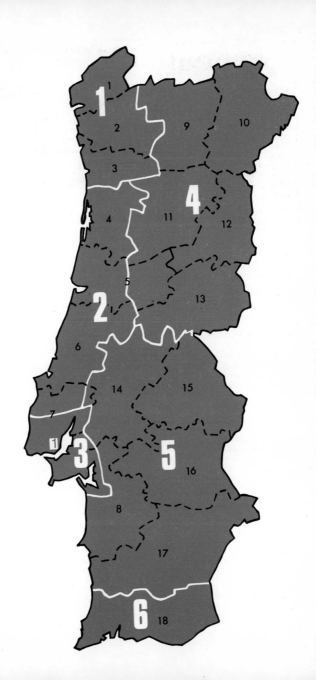

# PORTUGAL

This lovely country, which shares the Iberian Peninsula with Spain and Gibraltar – and occupies about a fifth of it – is the most westerly part of Europe except for Ireland. It measures 560km/347mi from north to south and 220/136 at its widest part from east to west. It is a little more than twice the size of Switzerland but only half as big as the state of Oklahoma. It has no more than ten million inhabitants, about a quarter of them living in or near its three main towns, Lisbon, Porto and Setúbal. Each of these towns stands at the mouth of a major river – Lisbon on the Tejo, Porto on the Douro and Setúbal on the Sado. For administrative purposes the country is divided into 18 districts, and for the convenience of the holidaymaker the authorities have grouped these districts into six self-evident regions: Costa Verde (the Green Coast), Costa de Prata (the Silver Coast), Lisbon and the coasts around it, Montanhas (the Mountains), Planícies (the Plains) and Algarve. Portugal's proverbially mild winters characterize all the regions except the Mountains and the Plains, where it can be icy.

You will find a country of cobbled streets and miles of cobbled roads, each stone laid painstakingly by hand. You will see women washing clothes in the rivers or in communal *lavadoiros* in the village streets. They carry home the washing or the shopping or a pail of water on their heads. You will find a country of fascinating old-fashioned shops impossible to classify, with secondhand cookers sharing the window space with babies' clothes and windfall apples. In the cafés shoe-shine boys still seek out customers and in the city squares have whole rows of covered booths. You will notice that the Portuguese are great hand-shakers and you may well see a hand outstretched across the bank counter as you approach to change your money.

There are only six towns with more than 40,000 inhabitants. The rest are smaller, homely places and in them lies part of the secret of the country's charm. Its farms and factories are small too. It is common to see a man and his mule cultivating the family's few acres while his wife looks after the chickens and pigs. There are 800,000 of these so-called subsistence farmers, producing enough for their needs but very little more, and using implements and methods their ancestors used over the centuries. Even on the plains of Alentejo resistance to modernization restricts yields of maize and cereals to only half the yield on similar land in neighbouring Spain and to less than a quarter of that in the rest of Europe. This means that half the country's grain has to be imported, most coming from the United States. It is the thousands of small farmers who grow the grapes and together make Portugal the fourth largest producer of wine in Europe. Her output reaches the astronomical figure of ten million hectolitres, which is a thousand million litre bottles. One tenth of this – one million hectolitres – is exported and the US takes a third, Switzerland a fifth and the UK well down the list nowadays with only a twentieth.

Portugal's industry is also, in the main, a composite of small units. Textiles, for example, which account for a third of the country's exports, come from no fewer than 1700 separate firms, 1280 of them employing under 50 people. It is the same with footwear. Its good quality and elegant design earn it high praise abroad. Here 1000 little factories employ an average of 30 people. And cork, of which Portugal is the world's biggest producer, gives work to a total of 20,000 people distributed among 600 separate factories. You will find the gnarled cork oak trees everywhere and see where the bark has been stripped from the trunks. (It is stripped every nine or ten years.)

These small personalized units, by resisting amalgamation, have helped to preserve the country's craftsmanship. There are few other countries in Europe where handmade articles can be seen in such attractive profusion. Every village has its potters, weavers, embroiderers, or its makers of lace, baskets, carpets, stools, shawls, mats, copperwork, leatherwork, filigree work, or ox yokes, harness, or artistic wrought iron. You will see these varied, colourful wares best at weekly markets or annual fairs and you may be sure that they have not been imported from Hong Kong.

Some of the highly-skilled crafts – filig-

ree work, for example, or the making of *azulejos* (small glazed tiles) – were learnt 1000 years ago from the Moors, that incredibly enlightened and cultured North African race who overran the whole Iberian Peninsula in the 8th century and stayed, at any rate in the Spanish part, till 1492. In Portugal their occupation was 250 years shorter, which in some ways was Portugal's loss, for the Moors left none of those unique architectural treasures which Spain inherited. On the other hand this country the Romans called Lusitania has been free and independent longer – for more than 800 years. During the whole of that time there has been an uninterrupted tradition of friendship with Britain. English archers helped Portugal's João I at the great battle of Aljubarrota (1385). This same João took an English wife, Philippa of Lancaster (1387), and Charles II of England (1662) a Portuguese one, Catharine of Bragança. England's Queen Elizabeth sent her army and navy to castigate the Spaniards who had seized Portugal and occupied it from 1580–1640, and Portugal and Britain fought side by side against Napoleon in the Peninsular War (1808–14). In World War I Portugal was on the side of the allies and in World War II, though neutral, made the Azores available to British shipping in the Battle of the Atlantic. No wonder Winston Churchill referred to Portugal, with pride, as 'Britain's oldest ally'.

Portugal was once – and indeed until very recently – one of the world's great colonial powers. Its empire was discovered and occupied by such men as Bartolomeu Dias, Diogo Cão, Vasco da Gama and Pedro Álvares Cabral, all of whom set out in their tiny caravels to explore beyond the boundaries of the known world. The brain and inspiration behind their voyages was Prince Henry the Navigator (1394–1460), one of the most outstanding men in Portuguese history. He was the son of João I and Philippa of Lancaster and therefore half English. At his famous school of navigation (see

Sagres) he trained his mariners and personally financed their voyages. His vision was validated during his lifetime but the greatest successes, including the discovery of Brazil, came after his death. Madeira was reached in 1419, the Azores in 1427 and Cape Bojador, on the west coast of Africa 800 miles from home, in 1434. Guinea was discovered in 1446, the Cape Verde Islands in 1456, Santo Tomé in 1470, Angola 1482, the Cape of Good Hope, affording a new route to India without passing through the pirate-infested Mediterranean, in 1486, Mozambique 1498, Brazil 1500, Goa and Macao ten years later and then Ceylon. It was indeed an enormous empire. But competition between Spain and Portugal in the Americas became so intense that Pope Alexander IV, called in as umpire, drew a vertical line '370 leagues west of the Cape Verde Islands', which gave Portugal Brazil and Spain just about all the rest. Distrust of Spain has always been deeply felt. The many hilltop castles you see guarding the border against Spanish invasion are evidence of this. 'From Spain,' says the Portuguese proverb, 'neither fair wind nor good marriage.' Perhaps it is not really true, unless it took Portuguese kings a long time to learn – for 17 of the 28 brides they married between 1174 and 1792 were Spanish and one, at least, Isabel of Aragón, became a saint.

Portugal's greatest disaster was the earthquake of 1755. It caused more material destruction than all her many wars together. It was one of the most devastating earthquakes ever known. But for it, the capital, Lisbon, would have far more old buildings of architectural interest than it has today. The remarkable thing is that it has any at all. The same can be said for many places around it. George Borrow, on his way to sell Bibles in Spain, was surprised to be told by an old lady at Elvas, 175km/108mi away, that she still remembered the priest being knocked down and the host falling to the floor. In fact the earthquake shook an area four times the size of Europe. Its centre was under the sea just off Lisbon and the waves it produced were detected along the American coast. In Scotland the waters of Loch Lomond rose two feet.

In 1910 the Portuguese monarchy came to an end after an existence of 721 years and the country for the first time in its history became a republic. During the next 16 years it had 45 different governments, many of them militarily imposed. In 1932 António de Oliveira Salazar, an economist who had been called in four years earlier to put the country's finances in order, became prime minister. He remained in office, heading an authoritative, police-backed, pro-Catholic government, for 34 years, despite five attempted *coups* and one attempted assassination. He resigned in 1968 through ill-health. He was succeeded by Marcelo Caetano whose introduction of democratic freedoms was too slow for many people. At the same time guerrilla leaders were gaining strength in the colonies, most of which were either seized or granted their independence. Three-quarters of a million colonial expatriates returned home. On 25 April 1974 an army general, António Spínola, took power in an almost bloodless coup. This was the famous *revolução dos cravos*, the carnation revolution, with happy-looking soldiers wearing flowers in their caps and helmets. The euphoria was curtailed by a communist-led takeover and the immediate nationalization of half the country's resources (including golf courses). But the inherent good sense of the people soon restored moderation, and Portugal today is a stable country which will probably be in the EEC by the time these words are in print. She has for many years been in NATO.

It would not be correct to call the Portuguese a merry people. It would be equally wrong to judge them by their national folkloric song, the *fado*, which has been described as the saddest music in the world. Nor are they a lively, martial people even though da Sousa, that great American master of military marches, was of Portuguese extraction. Rather, they are a gentle, kind, soft-spoken and courteous people. They say of themselves that Coimbra sings, Braga prays, Lisbon enjoys itself and Porto works. It would never occur to them to add that the national characteristic of genuine hospitality is common to all. For the visitor its discovery is a pleasure in store.

## Painting

Portugal has never produced any painters of world renown, but Velázquez (1599–1660) and Claudio Coello (1624–93), though Spanish by birth, were of Portuguese extraction. One Portuguese painter, **Nuno Gonçalves**, would probably have gained equal fame had more of his work survived. It is not known when he was born or when he died but the approximate dates are 1430–80. His most outstanding known work is the six-panelled *Adoration of St Vincent* in the Museum of Ancient Art in Lisbon. It is filled with striking, almost life-size, portraits of Prince Henry the Navigator and many of his contemporaries. For this work alone he is considered to be the greatest painter of his race.

**Vasco Fernandes** (1480–c1543), Portugal's foremost portrait painter of the 16th century, earned himself the title of *o Grão Vasco* (the Great Vasco) which didn't, however, prevent his dying poor. He founded the school of painting at Viseu. From Lisbon **Gaspar Vaz** (d.1568) joined him and they worked closely together, sometimes apparently on the same picture. Another painter was **Josefa de Óbidos** (1634–84). She was immensely versatile and included etching, terra-cotta modelling, silverwork, and calligraphy in her output. At a very early age she moved from Sevilla (her mother's home) and spent the rest of her life in Portugal. She ran a school of painting and, because the work attributed to her varies so widely in quality, it has been suggested that some of it is by her pupils. In more recent times **Silva Porto** (1850–93), **José Malhoa** (1855–1933), painter of country fairs, and **Amadeo de Sousa Cardoso** (1887–1918), friend of Modigliani, gained some fame in Europe.

## Literature

There is no doubt that Portugal's greatest writer was **Luís de Camoens** or Camões (1524–80). His *Amphitriões* was acted while he was still at university. His *Rimas* (rhymes) were passionate protestations that marriage to the girl he loved (Catarina de Ataide, one of the queen's ladies-in-waiting, to whom, it was said, 'he remained true till her death' many years later) should have been forbidden by her father. But his greatest work, which brought him world fame (though he followed the custom by dying poor), was *Os Lusiados* (*The Lusiads* or *The Lusitanians*). He wrote it in 1558 at the age of 34 though it was not published until 14 years later. It is the great Portuguese national epic and was only by a miracle saved from destruction. Camoens was shipwrecked on returning from Goa and floated ashore on a plank desperately clutching the precious manuscript. He wrote 352 sonnets (many published after his death), several songs and three dramas. Second in renown to Camoens is **Manuel Maria Barbosa du Bocage** (1765–1805). His sonnets are considered to be the best in the Portuguese language. For his liberal ideas he several times found himself in trouble with the Inquisition. In poetry, **Gil Vicente** (c1465–c1536) was the first to win renown. He wrote in both Portuguese and Spanish. His works included 44 highly original dramas, comedies, and farces, in addition to devotional works. Sometimes he composed the music too. The poet **Francisco Sá de Miranda** (1485–1558), who also wrote in Portuguese and Spanish, was the son of a canon at Coimbra University and was himself professor of law there. Other well-known Portuguese writers: **João Batista de Almeida Garrett** (1799–1854), epic poet, lyricist, dramatist and historical novelist, whose collected works filled 25 volumes. **Alexandre Herculano** (1810–77), poet, historical novelist and author of a four-volume history of Portugal. In 1828–32 he lived in Paris and London 'to escape the despotism of King Manuel'. **José Maria Eça de Queirós** (1845–1900), novelist.

## Architecture

The main distinctive contribution Portugal has made to architecture is the style which became known as **Manueline**, named after Manuel I (1495–1521). It was a florid, exuberant, highly decorative style which caught the national mood at the time of the great colonial discoveries. With its twisted stone columns and corbels, its stone tree trunks, ropes, anchors, knots, sails, seaweed, or even artichokes it was quite different from anything that had gone before. The best examples are the Convent of Christ at Tomar and the Hieronymite Monastery at Lisbon. It seems, however, to have been invented by a Frenchman, or at any rate an artist of French extraction, by the name of **Boytac**, of whom little is known except that he died about 1528. **Mateus Fernandes** (c1470–c1520) developed the

style and put it into operation, for he was also a master builder. The two brilliant **Arruda brothers**, Diogo (d.1535) and Francisco (d.1547) were the most outstanding of later Manueline architect-designers, sometimes introducing Moorish motifs (as in the Tower of Belém, Lisbon).

**Azulejos** Another distinctive characteristic of Portuguese architecture is the enthusiastic use of *azulejos*, the small glazed tiles that were originally blue (*azul*) but from the 17th century became multi-coloured and instead of geometric patterns bore artistic scenes. Wherever you go you will see *azulejos* covering the walls of buildings, sometimes whole streets of houses, even whole churches inside and out. The tiles were imported from Spain, then Holland but since the 17th century have been made in Portugal.

**Pillories** (*pelourinhos*), which are to be found in profusion throughout Portugal (especially in the northern half), are often veritable works of art and craftsmanship. They consist of a vertical column, sometimes twisted in the best Manueline tradition, set in a stepped stone base and capped with a decorative sculpture such as symbolic scales of justice or a weather-vane. It was no doubt considered that the miscreant, handcuffed to the column and thus exposed to public ridicule, would surely be consoled by the elegance of his surroundings.

*Cloisters, Hieronymite Monastery, Lisbon*

# PAPERWORK

## Passports

Visitors from the UK, the USA, Canada, and Australia must carry a current passport but do not require a visa. They are allowed to stay in the country 60 days (90 days for Australians) but not engage in professional or business activity. This period may be extended by applying to the Portuguese Registration Services (*Policía de Segurança Pública* or district police headquarters in any town) seven days before expiry.

Nationals of countries with which Portugal has no diplomatic relations need visas in addition to passports.

**UK citizens** should obtain well in advance (at least a month) a passport application form from any post office and take it or post it, together with the photographs, documents and fee specified on the form, to one of the passport offices whose addresses are given. In Northern Ireland forms are available only from the Passport Office, Belfast.

**US citizens** If you have not held a US passport during the past eight years you must apply in person, presenting a completed form DSP-11 ('Passport Application') together with fees and proof of American citizenship, to the passport office at Boston, Chicago, Detroit, Houston, Los Angeles, Miami, New Orleans, New York, Philadelphia, San Francisco, Seattle, Stamford, or Washington D.C. or to one of the several thousand federal or state courts or to one of the post offices that accept such applications. If you have had a previous passport you should apply on form DSP-82 ('Application for Passport by Mail') and post it, together with your previous passport, to one of the passport agencies in the cities mentioned above. The US authorities advise you to apply 'a few months' in advance of your planned departure.

**Canadian citizens** should obtain a passport application form from their local post office and mail it, with proof of Canadian citizenship (*eg* birth or naturalization certificate or previous passport) and fee to Passport Office, Dept. of External Affairs, 125 Sussex Drive, Ottawa, Ontario. Or they may present the application personally at the regional passport office in Calgary, Fredericton, Halifax, Hamilton, London, Montreal, Quebec, St John's, Saskatoon, Toronto, Vancouver, Victoria, Windsor or Winnipeg.

**All visitors** are advised to carry their passport with them at all times. They will need it when booking into hotels, changing money or travellers' cheques, collecting mail or in case of accident. If your passport is lost or stolen you should immediately contact your nearest consulate. (Useful Addresses p. 24.)

## Insurance

It is most important to have adequate insurance in case of illness or personal accident while in Portugal or on the way there or back. Medical and hospital treatment abroad can be extremely costly. On the other hand, insurance cover for short periods is extremely cheap. Your travel agent will be able to attend to it when you make your holiday arrangements. Alternatively, see any insurance broker. The usual policy covers medical expenses up to a stated limit and cash payments for permanent injury or death. Very often also it covers loss or theft of baggage, personal liability to third parties, expenses resulting from cancellation or curtailment of the holiday and loss of money up to a reasonable amount. There are no reciprocal health agreements between Portugal and the USA or Canada. UK visitors, however, are entitled to treatment by the Portuguese medical-social services but they must obtain form E111 from their local social security office in advance. (You should also ask for explanation leaflet SA28.) If you have a private health insurance it is advisable to check that it is valid abroad.

**Drivers:** see If You Are Motoring, p. 14.

**On entering Portugal** you may take with you unlimited amounts of money (Portuguese escudos or other currencies) only if it is in the form of travellers' cheques or drafts drawn on foreign banks. *In Portuguese bank notes or coins the maximum is 1000 escudos.* In addition UK citizens can take for their personal consumption 200 cigarettes or 100 cigarillos or 50 cigars or 150 gr tobacco. Citizens of USA, Canada or other non-European countries may take in double these amounts. All visitors can take in two cameras and one small cine-camera each with two rolls of film, one pair of binoculars, one record player with ten records, one portable recording machine, one portable TV set, one portable typewriter, one canoe less than 5.5m/18ft long and two pairs of skis. All these items must have been used.

**Weapons and ammunition**. Visitors intending to shoot game or take part in shooting competitions may take in up to six guns and 400 cartridges on depositing 1000 escudos refundable on leaving the country.

**Pets** may be imported but must be accompanied by a health certificate signed by a recognized veterinary surgeon and authenticated by a Portuguese consul in the applicant's country. If more than four months old the animal must have been vaccinated against rabies and the certificate must confirm that this has been done. Certificates in any language other than Portuguese, English or French must have a translation attached.

**Plants** or parts of plants from outside Europe need a special authorization from the Portuguese sanitary authorities.

# CUSTOMS

**On leaving Portugal** you may take with you a maximum of 1000 escudos in notes and coins, foreign currency up to the value of 25,000 escudos, or more if you can prove that you took it in, plus unused drafts or travellers' cheques issued to you outside Portugal.

**On returning home UK citizens** Drugs, firearms, flick knives, horror comics, uncooked meat and poultry and plants are strictly prohibited.

**US citizens** No tobacco or alcohol may be mailed back. Before buying a motor vehicle with the intention of taking it back to the States you are strongly advised to get a copy of the leaflet *Importing a Car*

issued by US Customs, Washington, D.C.20229, (202 566 8157). There are controls on the importation of pets (you can get a copy of *Pets, US Wildlife* from US Customs) firearms, plants, livestock, and poultry. Narcotics and dangerous drugs are absolutely forbidden.

**Canadian citizens** As exemption from import duty depends upon the length and frequency of absences as well as on cost of purchases Canadian Customs and Excise recommend you to keep dated bills and receipts, even for accommodation. Once every calendar quarter you may take in with you goods to the value of Can.$50 and once every calendar year an additional Can.$150-worth provided the trips are separate. As part of each exemption (but minimum age limit 16): 200 cigarettes *and* 50 cigars *and* 0.91/2lb tobacco *plus* 1.1 litres wine or liqueur *or* 8.2 litres/288 fl oz ale or beer. For information about importing motor vehicles or firearms consult local customs office or about pets or plants Department of Agriculture, Ottawa, Ontario K1A 0C5.

**USA and Canada** You should also, before you leave, get your local customs office to record valuables such as cameras, radios, sporting goods you intend to take with you to facilitate their readmission.

| **Duty-free allowances** *subject to change* | | | Bought duty free or outside EEC | Duty and tax paid in EEC |
|---|---|---|---|---|
| Tobacco | | Cigarettes or | 200 | 300 |
| | | Cigars *small* or | 100 | 150 |
| | | Cigars *large* or | 50 | 75 |
| | | Pipe tobacco | 250 gm | 400 gm |
| Alcohol | Spirits *over 38.8° proof* or | | 1 litre | 1½ litres |
| | Fortified or sparkling wine plus | | 2 litres | 3 litres |
| | Table wine | | 2 litres | 4 litres |
| Perfume | | | 50 gm | 75 gm |
| Toilet water | | | 250 cc | 375 cc |
| Other goods | | | £28 | £120 |

*(Tobacco note box:)* Double if you live outside Europe

US customs permit duty-free $300 retail value of purchases per person, 1 quart of liquor per person over 21, and 100 cigars per person.

# CURRENCY

The Portuguese unit of currency is the *escudo*, which is divided into 100 *centavos*. The symbol $ is used to separate the escudos from the centavos. In other words it is used as a decimal point. Thus ten escudos and 50 centavos are written 10$50. There are bank notes for 20, 50, 100, 500 and 1000 escudos and coins of 50 centavos (written very confusingly $50), one escudo (1$00), 2½ escudos (2$50), five escudos (5$00), ten escudos (10$00) and 25 escudos (25$00). Foreign currency and travellers' cheques may be changed at banks, hotels and at the better shops. (You will be intrigued to find that one of the banks is called the Bank of the Holy Spirit, *Banco del Espírito Santo*).

**Bank opening hours** are 0830–1145 and 1300–1435 Monday to Friday but in summer, at Christmas and Easter there is a currency exchange service all day and every day at the main resorts, at airports and at frontier posts.

**Travellers' cheques** are cashable at a somewhat higher rate than bank notes and are, of course, much safer to carry. For currency restrictions on entry and departure see Customs, p. 11.

**Credit cards** British, but not North American cards, are usable for drawing money from banks. British travellers wishing to cash personal cheques will need a special Eurocheque card supplied by their own banks. Money wired from the US or Canada to a Portuguese bank usually takes two–three days to arrive.

# HOW TO GET THERE

**By Air** Portugal has three international airports – Lisbon, Porto (Costa Verde) and Faro (Algarve). Many of the major airlines provide direct, non-stop flights to Lisbon. They include British Airways, British Caledonian, Canadian Pacific, Pan American, South African Airways and Trans World, in addition to Portugal's own airline TAP. Flying time from New York or Montreal is about seven hours. From London there are daily direct flights (in summer several) to the Portuguese airports. Flights from UK provincial cities call at either Heathrow or Gatwick.

**By Sea** It is possible to travel from New York to Lisbon or Porto but as the sailings are infrequent information should be sought from a knowledgeable travel agent. From the UK there is no regular service by sea at the present time, though many of the cruise liners put in at Lisbon.

**By Coach** There is a service of air-conditioned coaches between London and Lisbon five days a week. Travelling time is 46 hrs. Details from: British Railways Travel Centre, 4 Lower Regent Street, London SW1, or Europabus (Overseas) Inc., 630 Fifth Avenue, New York 10020.

**By Car** The total distance by road from the French Channel coast to the Portuguese border, taking the route Boulogne, Rouen, Évreux, Chartres, Tours, Poitiers, Angoulême, Bordeaux, Irún (Spain), San Sebastián, Vitoria, Burgos, Valladolid, Salamánca, Fuentes de Oñoro, is roughly 1600km/1000mi. As an alternative to motoring all the way there is a twice-weekly car ferry (Brittany Ferries) from Plymouth to Santander (Spain). The crossing time is 24 hours, and from Santander to the same point on the Portuguese border (Fuentes de Oñoro) the distance is 470km/290mi. An all-inclusive organized motoring holiday, using your own car, with all accommodation reserved for you in advance in a series of *pousadas* with a more restful week or so in a seaside apartment and including the Plymouth-Santander crossing, is offered by Lisbon Promotions Ltd., 13 Sandyford Place, Glasgow G3 7NB. As a further alternative, it is possible to take your car by train. (See By Train, below.)

**By Train** You can go all the way from London to Lisbon by train with a change only at Paris, the scheduled travelling time being about 38 hours. Sleeping car accommodation is available on the *Sud Express* from the Spanish frontier only but couchettes are provided from Paris to both Lisbon and Porto. There are reduced (limited availability) holiday return fares and discounts of around 40% for senior citizens. Young people up to 26 in the USA and Canada and other non-European countries can obtain reduced-price Eurailpass tickets valid for Portuguese and all other West European railways. They must obtain them in their own country before leaving. Cars may accompany passengers from Boulogne to Biarritz and again, after the short drive to the Spanish frontier at Hendaye/Irún, to Madrid. From there one drives on to Portugal. Further information from travel agents or Sealink Travel Ltd, Continental Travel Centre, Liverpool Street Station, London, EC2.

**By all-inclusive holiday** This method is certainly the cheapest and most trouble-free, because the fare (by air, coach, train or other means) accommodation and delivery right to the door are all included, sometimes for less than the normal fare alone. 'Fly-drive' holidays are very popular, with a car awaiting you at the airport and accommodation in hotel, villa or apartment. Or there is a 'fly-coach' holiday (Thompson Holidays, Greater London House, Hampstead Road, London, NW1) including flight from one of seven UK provincial cities and a coach tour of Portugal's showplaces. Travel agents have details of these and other schemes, and of 'activity holidays'. (See Enjoy Yourself, p. 00.)

# INTERNAL TRAVEL

**By Air** The Portuguese airline TAP provides a regular service between Lisbon and the following places: Porto (Costa Verde), Bragança, Covilhã and Viseu (Montanhas) and Faro, Portimão and Vila Real de Santo António (Algarve). Fares and times of flights can be obtained from any travel agent.

**Boats and ferries** From **Lisbon**, starting from Praça do Comércio (also called Terreiro do Paço) there is a very frequent service of passenger ferries (no cars) across the River Tejo to Cacilhas/Almada, Barreiro, Seixal and Montijo on the south bank. Starting from Cais do Sodré, a few hundred metres west of Praça do Comércio, there are ferries for passengers and cars to Trafaria and Porto Brandão. Any of these trips is worthwhile for the enjoyment of sightseeing even if the destination doesn't particularly interest you. From June to September the town councils of Lisbon and Almada jointly run trips on the river lasting five hours with lunch at Cacilhas. From **Setúbal** there are frequent passenger and car ferries across the wide estuary of the River Sado to Tróia beach. A hovercraft does the same trip. In the **Algarve** local river ferries operate from Faro, Tavira, and Portimão. From Vila Real de Santo António there is a service of passenger and car ferries across the River Guadiana to the Spanish town of Ayamonte. From **Caminha** (Costa Verde) in the very north of the country a small passenger ferry (no cars) crosses the lovely River Minho which separates Portugal from Spain. From **Porto** every day except Monday a comfortable launch leaves the quay of Cais da Ribeira (near the Don Luis bridge) for a sightseeing trip on the River Douro. Along the whole coast there are local boat trips.

**By Rail** Portuguese Railways (CP) serve practically the whole country. From Lisbon to Cascais and Sintra there is a specially good service. The express trains *Rápidos* or *Direitos* take about three hours Lisbon–Porto and four hours Lisbon–Faro. On all CP lines there is a discount for groups of ten or more persons. There are also 'kilometre booklets' at special rates for a total of 3000km over a maximum period of three months, and 'tourist tickets' valid for seven, 14 or 21 days. There are half-price tickets for those over 65 travelling a minimum of 50km. You can take your car on some trains between Lisbon and Porto, Castelo Branco, Régua (Vila Real) and Guarda. CP also have two 'vintage steam trains' which are operated for tourists whenever the demand is sufficient. They are both in the Costa Verde region. One, called the '19th-century train', consists of a British locomotive of 1875 with Portuguese, French and Swiss carriages and runs between Porto and Valença. The other, the 'historic train', with a German locomotive of 1905 and German, French and Portuguese carriages, runs on the narrow-gauge line beside the River Tâmega between Livração, Amarante, and Arco de Baúlhe.

**Local buses** All the main towns are connected to each other by road services,

some direct and therefore speedy, others calling at smaller towns and villages on the way. The excellent modern coaches of *Rodoviaria Nacional* RN operate throughout the whole country.

**Taxis** are available in all the main towns and are painted green and black. They all carry a list of fares (which must be produced to the customer on request) in Portuguese, English and French. For luggage weighing more than 30kg the additional charge is half the fare shown on the taxi meter. In the smaller towns where there are no taxi ranks there are nevertheless cars which operate as taxis and charge by the km.

**Excursions** Innumerable half-day, whole-day or several-day organized tours are available in all the main holiday areas, the majority operating only in summer but some all the year round. Information is best obtained from travel agents, tourist offices, or hotel porters.

# IF YOU ARE MOTORING

**Documents** (1) A valid driving licence issued in your own country. A provisional licence is not acceptable. But please note that to cross Spain you need an international driving permit obtainable in the UK, USA and Canada from motoring organizations. (For addresses see below).

(2) The vehicle registration book. If you are not the owner of the vehicle or the owner's husband, wife or 'a relative to the first degree', you should have the owner's written authority to use it. If the vehicle is hired outside Portugal the hirers should provide you with a 'hire car registration

certificate'. (3) A 'green card' issued by the insurers of the vehicle. Don't forget to check that your insurance is valid while the vehicle is aboard sea or river ferries or being transported by train. Though not obligatory it is advisable (especially if passing through Spain) to have a 'bail bond', issued by the vehicle's insurers. This acts as a guarantee in the event of serious accident involving personal injury to third parties. (4) A nationality plate (GB, USA, CANADA, etc) must be affixed to the rear of the vehicle and caravan or trailer.

**Children** under 12 are not allowed to travel in the front seats.

**Seat belts** must be worn by front seat passengers (in France and Spain too).

**Fines** can be imposed on the spot for all infractions.

**Minimum age** for driving a car or motorcycle over 125cc is 18.

**Roads** Some are excellent but most are adequate for leisurely sight-seeing rather than for high-speed motoring.

**Speed limits** for passenger vehicles not exceeding 3500kg/7700lb and motorcycles without side-car: in built-up areas 60kph/37mph, in open country 90/56, on motorways 120/74. Any variations (surprising few) of these general rules are indicated by the standard Continental sign, ie black figures (meaning maximum kph) on white circle with red border. But please note that on some Portuguese roads there are **minimum** speed limits and these are indicated by white figures on a blue background. You will find them chiefly on the motorways (40kph/25mph) but on the 25 Abril Bridge across the River Tejo at Lisbon the minimum is 30kph/18mph and the maximum 60/37.

**Motorways** charge a toll (in France and Spain too).

**New drivers** (under one year) are limited to 90kph/56mph on motorways and must display a '90' disc (obtainable from office of Automobile Club de Portugal at frontier).

**Headlamps** which are not adjusted for right-hand driving should be fitted with an adaptor.

**Rules of the road** Drive on the right, overtake on the left and give preference to traffic emerging from the right in built-up areas and at crossings. Most of the road signs are international but some are in words, such as: *cruzamento* = crossroads; *desvio* = diversion; *entrada* = entrance; *obras* = road works; *pedestres* or *peões* = pedestrians; *perigo* = danger; *posto do socorros* = first aid post; *saida* = exit; *sentido proibido* = no entry; *sentido único* = one way.

**Parking** You are allowed to park for an indefinite time unless there is any indication to the contrary.

**Ambulance service** Dial 115 from any telephone in the country at any time of day or night. You should give the exact position of accident, number of persons injured, vehicles involved, if there are people trapped and if there is a fire. Alternatively, the nearest roadside orange-coloured SOS telephone may be used, free, by pressing the button and waiting a few seconds for the operator to answer. If the operator does not speak English and your own Portuguese is inadequate it is very likely that other persons involved, or a passing motorist, will take over.

**Warning triangle** must be carried and in case of accident, breakdown or puncture must be placed 50m/55yd back along the road.

**Fuel** (*gasolina*) and oil (*óleo*): most international brands are on sale but there are only two grades of *gasolina*: *normal* (85 octane) and *super* (98 octane). As filling stations are few and far between away from the main roads it is advisable to keep the tank well topped up.

**Spare parts** Even though the major car manufacturers have their distributors and agents throughout Portugal, it can still save time and delay to carry a spare parts kit. These can nowadays be hired before leaving home and any parts remaining unused returned.

**Motoring organizations** supply spare parts kits to their members. They will also take care of all the documentation of an overseas trip, make ferry and motorail bookings, attend to insurance, recommend routes and come to the rescue in case of breakdown.

**UK** Automobile Association, Fanum House, Basingstoke, Hants; Royal Automobile Club, 89–91 Pall Mall, London, SW1; Royal Scottish Automobile Club, 17 Rutland Square, Edinburgh.

**USA** American Automobile Association, 8111 Gatehouse Road, Falls Church, Virginia 22042.

**Canada** Canadian Automobile Association, 1775 Courtwood Crescent, Ottawa K2C 3J2.

They all have reciprocal assistance agreements with the Automóvel Club de Portugal, Rua Rosa Araújo 24 Lisbon (563931), Rua Gonçalo Cristóvão 2–6, Porto (29271) and offices throughout the country.

**Car hire** Portuguese and international companies offer cars for hire for short or longer periods. This can be arranged at the airports and at offices in the main towns. Big discounts are often available off-season, so it is best to shop around.

# ACCOMMODATION

**Hotels** Portugal is well equipped nowadays to offer whatever type of accommodation the visitor requires, from the luxurious to the very economical. The international system of stars is used to denote category. The main types of accommodation are: hotels (one to five stars), apartment hotels (two to four stars), *estalagems* or high quality inns (four to five stars), *albergarias* (all four stars) and *pensões* or pensions (one to four stars). In addition there are motels (two to three stars) and government-owned *pousadas* which are either newly built or occupying former palaces, monasteries, or castles. In *pousadas* a stay is limited to five days. Except for one star and two star *pensões* all establishments have some rooms with private bath. The word *residencial* or just the letter R in the hotel sign means that the establishment has no dining room and offers bed and breakfast only. A complete list of accommodation in any area can be obtained from any tourist information office inside Portugal or from Portuguese National Tourist Offices abroad. (See Useful Addresses, p. 24.)

Prices for all accommodation and meals are controlled and must be clearly displayed in all bedrooms. You will notice that minimum and maximum prices are given. The minimum applies to the low season, maximum to the high season. The price of a room includes Continental breakfast (bread or toast with butter and jam; tea or coffee). If a double room is occupied by one person only the price of the breakfast will be deducted. (The breakfast price must appear in the list displayed.) There is an extra charge of ten percent for meals (except breakfast) served in the room. *Pensões* (but not hotels) which have a dining room may charge 20 percent extra on the room price if a guest eats out, but only if he stays more than two nights. (If you enjoy trying different restaurants you can avoid this surcharge by choosing an R (*residencial*) pension as explained above.) All prices include service and taxes (but see Tipping, p. 24). There are reductions for children under eight. Rooms must be vacated by 12 noon on day of departure. All establishments have an official complaints book (*livro de reclamações*) which must be produced on request. Complaints may also be made at tourist information offices or direct to the directorate-general of tourism (address below).

For visitors who like to get to know the country and the people a little more intimately, accommodation is often available in private houses or farms. Details can be obtained from: Direcção-Geral do Turismo, Avenida António Augusto de Aguiar 86, Lisboa.

**Apartments** Tremendous development has taken place in the last few years, especially in the Algarve, where the big tour operators make block bookings and offer all-inclusive holidays, mostly by air but sometimes by coach. For winter use some of the apartments have heating (which is needed when the sun goes down) and heated swimming pools. But many agents, both inside and outside Portugal, cater for visitors travelling independently. Information is best obtained from travel agents or from advertisements that appear frequently in the press.

**Camping** Portugal has 100 camping sites, two-thirds of them on or near the coast. They are classified with one to four stars according to the facilities they offer. You are encouraged to use only these official sites. It is permitted, however, to camp elsewhere provided the position you choose is not (a) within one km of an official camping site or of 'beaches or other places frequented by the public' or (b) in an urban centre. The total number of persons (not just your party) at any one site must not exceed 20. Many of the official sites have modern installations sometimes including a restaurant or a supermarket. Tents and other equipment, including trailers, can be hired from the motoring organizations in the UK. Further information about all these matters, with a comprehensive guide to existing sites entitled *Roteiro Campista*, can be obtained from tourist offices or from Federação Portuguesa de Campismo e Caravanismo, Rua Voz do Operário l-r/c esq., 1100 Lisboa.

**Youth Hostels** There is one in Lisbon, one in Porto and nine more dotted about the country in attractive situations. They are available for young people only, age limits 14 to 40, who must, however, be members of the Youth Hostels Association in their own country and be able to produce their membership card. All the hostels provide sleeping accommodation, some provide meals and the rest have cooking facilities. Nearly all of them are open all the year. Further information together with a map showing where the hostels are situated is available from tourist offices or from: Associação Portuguesa de Pousadas de Juventud, Rua Andrade Corvo 46, Lisboa.

# FOOD AND DRINK

In general, the best Portuguese food is to be found in restaurants and not in hotels. There are two reasons for this. The first is that foreign visitors are inclined to look askance at unfamiliar dishes and thus hoteliers have been forced to produce a sort of internationalized cuisine that can offend nobody. The second reason is that meals included in full-board terms limit the chef's budget and inevitably cramp his style. So if you want to try typical Portuguese food, you need to go where the Portuguese themselves go – to a restaurant. These restaurants are immensely varied. Officially there are four categories: luxury (*luxo*), 1st class (*primeira*), 2nd class (*segunda*) and 3rd class (*terceira*). The *terceiras* are the bar-restaurant places known as *tascas*. There you get good food, plenty of it, no frills and, unless you are lucky, no table cloth. At the other end of the scale are the expensive establishments where you can naturally eat well but often in an atmosphere that is no more Portuguese than Park Lane or Manhattan. (For late-night restaurants with *fado* singing see Entertainment, p. 21). Wherever you eat you will discover that the Portuguese have enormous appetites and, ironically, the cheaper the restaurant the bigger the portion.

**Food** So what is there to eat? It has been said that half the Portuguese diet consists of *bacalhau*, which is cod, and the other half eggs, which are the main ingredients of their desserts. Well, it's very nearly true. Furthermore cod, their national dish, is not the fresh variety one would expect in a country with 830km/515mi of Atlantic coastline but is brought all the way from Newfoundland or from Norway and dried and salted. It looks unpleasant, it smells unpleasant and it has to be left to soak for several days before the cook can do anything with it. Nevertheless you will be surprised how good it is. The Portuguese will tell you there are 365 ways of serving it, to enable them to eat it every day without monotony. The favourite way is steamed with boiled potatoes, or slightly more elaborate, stewed with potatoes, eggs and olives (this is called *bacalhau à Gomes de Sá*) or, somewhat better still, served with a sauce of tomato, pimento and onion. There is also *bacalhau assado* (roast cod), *bacalhau à grelos* (with Brussels' sprouts) and *bacalhau com todos* ('with everything'). But, despite the Portuguese leg-pull, there are very many appetizing dishes apart from cod.

**Soups** The most popular is *caldo verde* (green soup) made of puréed potato, finely shredded cabbage and a slice or two of sausage. *Ensopada* is made from meat and bread; *grão* is chick-pea soup, *açorda* is made of fish and bread, *sopa rica da peixe* is a more elaborate fish soup. In hot weather try *gaspacho*, the delicious ice-cold soup to which chopped onions, pimentos, cucumber are added along with *croûtons* at the time of serving.

**Seafood** The so-called Portuguese oyster, although well-known abroad, is seldom eaten at home. But mussels (*mexilhões*) are good, either on their own or as part of some other dish. *Amêijoas* are clams and *amêijoas na cataplana* are clams cooked in a white sauce with ham, sausage, onion, tomato and paprika. The word *cataplana* really refers to the double copper pan used for cooking. Fresh sardines (*sardinhas*), though hardly a dish to be ordered in a restaurant, are delicious eaten with the fingers in a bar or straight from a street brazier. *Lampreias* or lampreys, those eel-like creatures you see in some Portuguese rivers clinging to rocks with their suction mouths, are worth trying if only because they are unusual. So are octopi (*polvos*) and squid (*lulas*), both of which you will also often find in *caldeira* or fish stew, which is another staple dish and a good one.

**Meat** The Portuguese are not great meat eaters but you may come across *bife na frigideira* or beef served in an earthenware dish with a wine and mustard sauce. Pork, much more popular than beef, comes mostly from open-range pigs that feed on cork oak acorns in the Alentejo plains. (You will sometimes detect the unmistakable nutty flavour in Portuguese hams and sausages.) But in Alentejo they often mix pork (first marinated) appetizingly with clams – *carne de porco à Alentejo*. *Paio* is smoked loin of pork rolled and cut into slices. Roast kid (*cabrito assado*) is similar to roast lamb but slightly richer. Both are often served with rice, a taste for which the Portuguese long ago acquired through their Indian colonies, along with *caril* (curry). But even more tempting is *leitão* or roast suckling pig.

**Desserts** Portuguese desserts based on egg yolk, sugar and often almonds (especially in Algarve) are legion. They range from *doces de ovos* (egg sweets) to *papas de freiras* (nuns' breasts). You will also probably notice that rice pudding is popular and so is *pudim flam* which is caramel cream. Something rather more 20th century is *pudim Molotov* (fluffy white of egg with a caramel sauce). To round off a meal you have a choice of many regional cheeses. The best of them is undoubtedly *queijo Serra da Estrela*, made of ewes' milk from the Estrela mountains. You might also try some of the goats' milk cheeses – *rabaçal* or *cabreiro* – or the fresh *requeijão*. And, of course, to go with the cheese there is nothing in the world better than a good port (for a note on which see below). But first you may like a Portuguese coffee (black, *bica* or *café simples*; white, *galão*) which they claim is, jointly with the Italian, the best in Europe.

**Drink** The authorities claim that tap water is perfectly all right to drink (though in Lisbon, especially, it tastes strongly of chlorine). Most people, however, drink bottled mineral water (*água mineral*) either still (*sem gás*) or carbonated (*com gás*). There are also orangeade (*laranjada*) and lemonade (*limonada*), good light lager-type beer (*cerveja*) and tea which goes by the homely name of *chá*. But obviously the thing to drink in Portugal is wine. Not satisfied with the three normal shades – white (*branco*), rosé (*rosado*) and red (*tinto*) – Portugal adds a fourth, green (*verde*). But the word describes its immaturity, not its colour. In fact you can have *vinho verde tinto* (green red wine). It is young wine of around 8–11 degrees of alcohol, still fermenting slightly in the bottle, and is grown, appropriately, inland from the Green Coast, the Costa Verde. It was the first of Portugal's wines to be exported – in the 15th century. The other well-known Portuguese wines are the Burgundy-type Dão, the dry white wine of Bucelas, the light white and red wines of Colares and a wide variety from the banks of the Tejo. It is interesting to try in their country of origin the Fonseca, Lancers and Aliança wines so popular in the States. There are also sparkling wines from Lamego and Bairrada and brandy (distilled from wine – it takes nine barrels of wine to make one of brandy). Good brands to try are Croft, '1920' and Casaleiro. The Portuguese liqueurs are also worth trying – *bagaceira*, distilled from grape skins and pips, *medronheira*, from the evergreen arbutus tree, and *cana*, from sugar cane. From Setúbal comes the sweet, fortified, dessert wine *moscatel*, made from black and white grapes mixed, and from Portugal's volcanic, holiday-resort Atlantic island of Madeira the famous wine of all the same name. But the most famous of all is *port*. It was always in the past an almost exclusively English drink but there is no longer any monopoly. Nowadays more than three times as much goes to France as to Britain. And the Portuguese themselves are acquiring a taste for it, though they prefer white port rather than red and as an *apéritif*. Gone also are the days when the grapes were trodden by the human foot. Now they are crushed mechanically and the *musto* is sealed up in metal or concrete tanks until the sugar content falls to the required level. Then the *musto* is run off and dosed with 20 percent its volume of brandy to stop further fermentation. It stays on the vineyard until the spring when tanker wagons carry it to the *armazens* or warehouses of Vila Nova de Gaia opposite Porto, where it is stored in huge vats holding 100,000 litres/22,000 imperial gallons/26,450 American gallons. Two years later the quality of the wine is assessed. If a vintage year is declared the port spends another 15 years in bottle and becomes a rich purple colour. Tawny port is left to mature for seven years in the barrel and loses much of its colour. The cheaper and sweeter ruby port is bottled at an earlier age and marketed straight away.

**Meal times** The normal time for lunch (*almoço*) is 1200–1430 and dinner (*jantar*) 1930–2130, or later at the *fado* restaurants, tea, at any time, at a *salão de chá*.

# ENJOY YOURSELF

**Disabled people** are catered for by Villas Portuguesas, a small family company, of 67 Marylebone High Street, London, W.1. Each holiday is planned according to the applicant's particular needs and can include all travel arrangements or simply accommodation in a selected villa, apartment or cottage.

**Fishing** At least 200 varieties of fish are to be found in Portuguese waters and, one way or another, can be caught. Even from the beach (preferably when the sea is rough or at night) there is every chance of landing sole, plaice, bream or bass weighing one or two kg. However, they are not easy. The Portuguese will remind you with a twinkle that they have been fishing these waters for centuries and have caught all the easy ones. There is also good fishing from rocks and from cliff tops (even from the top of Cape St Vincent) but this is extremely dangerous, as a sudden wave, a high wind or the slightest misjudgment can have fatal consequences. Fishing from a boat is much safer and more rewarding. Quite near the shore one can catch the bigger bass, groupers (both of which offer stiff resistance) and eels. Further out and at greater depth there are skate, mackerel, dolphins and tunny.

**Big game fishing** For the highest category of the sport one needs special equipment including a short, strong rod with a pulley at the end instead of an eye, and twisted nylon line. The catch then can be swordfish weighing 100–150kg/ 220–330lb (a Portuguese fisherman caught one weighing 352kg/775lb) and shark (record catch 262kg/576lb). The main centres for this type of fishing are Sesimbra (Lisbon Coast), Vilamoura and Portimão (Algarve). At all three places visiting enthusiasts can join the fishing trips that are regularly organized, and they can also buy the necessary equipment. Further information from tourist offices or from: Federação Portuguesa de Pesca Desportiva, Rua Arco do Cego 90, 5o, 1000 Lisbon.

**Golf** Portugal has no fewer than 15 golf courses – at Porto and Praia de Miramar (both Costa Verde), Vimeiro (Costa de Prata), Estoril (2), Lisbon (2) and Tróia (all Lisbon Region), Vidago (Montanhas) and Almansil (2), Lagos, Penina and Vilamoura (2) (all Algarve). The course at Porto, laid out in 1890, is the oldest in continental Europe after Pau, France. Among the courses' designers are such famous golfers as Henry Cotton, Frank Pennick, and Bill Mitchell. Full details of all the courses and of temporary membership for visitors can be obtained at Portuguese information offices or from Federação Portuguesa de Golfe, Avenida João Crisóstomo 6 R/C dto., 1000 Lisbon. There are also many all-inclusive golfing holidays with air travel and accommodation in good, conveniently situated hotels. Travel agents can provide details.

**Mountain climbing** This activity is not yet organized in Portugal, though there is a very helpful federation (Clube Nacional de Montanhismo, Rua Formosa 303, 2o, 4000 Porto) which is always ready to provide information for visitors and even to guide those who wish to explore such mountain ranges as Gerês, Marão or Estrela. The federation is only just starting on the ambitious task of mapping and signposting paths, shelters, water sources, possible camp sites and beauty spots. But it already has a slogan for its Saturday outings: 'A day on the march, a week of good health'.

**Cave exploring** is also in its infancy but about 20 local clubs (complete list obtainable from the secretary of the federation mentioned above) have so far been formed and visitors, especially those with experience, are welcomed.

**Walking** Ramblers Holidays Ltd., 13 Longcroft House, Fretherne Road, Welwyn Garden City, Herts., offer what they call 'a fairly easy walking holiday' based at the lovely Gerês National Park (Costa Verde) which extends over 700km²/270mi².

**Pilgrimages** Pilgrimage holidays to Fatima and district are organized by Mancunia Travel Ltd., 30 Brown Street, Manchester. There is a choice of air travel with local transport by coach in Portugal (eight days) or coach all the way from Manchester or London (11 days). There are normally six pilgrimages a year, to coincide with the processions of the 12th–13th of each month. (See Fatima, p. 38.) Bon Voyage Travel Ltd. of 2–3 Patrick Street, Dun Laoghaire, Dublin, can organize tours to Fatima for parish groups of a minimum of 30 persons.

**Riding** Portugal's climate and countryside are ideal for horseriding and there are many stables which cater for it. Experienced riders will find both the Portuguese Lusitano and the Anglo-Arab stocks. Learners are also provided for and there are ponies for children. Some of the stables near the coast advertize moonlight canters along the beach! All-inclusive holidays are available but as they are liable to change or discontinuation it is preferable to consult a travel agent. You could also write to Federação Equestre Portuguesa, Rua Arco do Cego 90, 5oD, 1000 Lisbon.

**Shooting** Visitors wishing to shoot in Portugal should, well before their visit, ask the Portuguese National Tourist Office in their own country for the current regulations. (See Useful Addresses p. 24 and Customs p. 11.) Among species it is permitted to shoot are pigeons, quail, duck, thrushes, starlings, rooks, partridges, pheasants, rabbits, foxes, wolves and wild boar. Hares, in danger of extinction, are strictly protected. The normal season runs from mid-Oct. to end-Feb. but shooting is permitted only on Sundays, Thursdays and public holidays. The government department responsible for game protection is the Direcção-Geral dos Serviços Florestais e Aquícolas, Avenida João Crisóstomo 26–28, Lisbon.

**Swimming** The Portuguese tourist authorities publish a map on which are indicated no fewer than 63 main beaches with a note (in English) about many smaller and quieter beaches nearby. A copy can be obtained from tourist information offices in Portugal or in other countries. (For addresses see p. 24.) Nude bathing is not allowed.

**Tennis** The best time to play tennis in the Portuguese climate is from September to May and in the early morning or late afternoon during the three hot months of

June to August. There are many courts throughout the country (mostly on the coast but some inland) which you can hire by the hour. At many places it is possible to hire racquets and balls and at some places coaching is available. All-inclusive holidays are offered by Caravela Tours, 38–44 Gillingham Street, London, SW1, and Portugal Holidays Ltd., 37 Ivor Place, London, NW1, in conjunction with the well-known 'tennis centre' at Vale do Lobo (Algarve) run personally by Roger Taylor, Britain's foremost player 1964–74 and winner of the US Open Doubles 1971 and 1972.

**Underwater fishing** The whole coast is good for diving but the Algarve waters are the most transparent. If you wish to practise **aqualung diving** you should note that you are not permitted to use a gun or any other fishing device. **Spearfishing** is allowed only when no artificial breathing apparatus is employed. Even so the minimum distance from the beach must be 50m and a marker buoy is obligatory. The waters around the Berlenga Islands, off Peniche (Costa de Prata) are a natural preserve and all kinds of fishing are prohibited. There is a **decompression chamber** at the Diving Wing of Alfeite Naval Base (Base Naval do Alfeite, Mergulhadores da Armada) across the river from Lisbon, and there are monoplace chambers at the local fire brigade of Vila Real de Santo António (Algarve) and Clube Internacional de Férias at Torralba (Setúbal-Tróia). Aqualung bottles can be refilled at various places. Further information from the National Federation of Underwater Activities (Federação Portuguesa de Actividades Subaquáticas, Rua Arco do Cego 90, 5o, 1096 Lisbon).

**University courses** for foreigners over 16 are available at Lisbon University. The summer course occupies the months of June and July, the annual course the last week October to 10 February and 27 February to end-May. No qualifications are required for entry but each course has three levels: elementary, (15 hrs a week language and laboratory), intermediate (10 hrs language and laboratory, four hrs Portuguese culture) and advanced (10 hrs grammar and language and 10 hrs Portuguese history, literature and geography). Students completing either course receive a certificate or a diploma. Details and list of fees from: Curso de Lingua e Cultura Portuguesa, Facultade de Letras, Cidade Universitária, 1699 Lisbon.

**Waterskiing, windsurfing** Portugal's many lagoons and reservoirs supplement her long coastline in providing exceptionally good conditions for both waterskiing and windsurfing. There are starting

ramps and hoists at many places. Equipment also may be hired and instruction is often available for beginners. Tourist information offices can inform on local facilities.

**Wine tasting** A visit to one of the main wine-producing areas can be the highlight of a holiday. Groups are organized from most of the tourist centres and details can be obtained from travel agents, information offices, or hotel porters. If you prefer to go independently to an *adega* or wine cellar you will be equally welcome. At Porto on the Costa Verde you could go to the cellars of Real Vinícola or to any of the 'wine lodges' bearing such famous names as Sandeman, Cockburn, Croft, all of which are at Vila Nova de Gaia across the river from the city; on the Costa de Prata to Caves Aliança, Vinícola de Sangalhos (Aveiro); in the Montanhas region to Mateus Rosé at Vila Real; in the Lisbon district to José Maria de Fonseca at Vila Nogueira de Azeitão (Setúbal); or in the Algarve to Adega Cooperativa de Lagoa at Lagoa. Alternatively, Blackheath Travel Ltd. of 13 Blackheath Village, London, SE3, organize several all-inclusive wine tasting tours to Portugal, flying from London Heathrow, staying in good hotels and visiting the vineyards and cellars. They take place in spring/early summer and again in autumn. Some cover the Porto district and Douro valley, the rest Cascais (Lisbon).

*A cavaleiro placing banderilhas*

**Bullfighting** in Portugal, unlike bullfighting in Spain, involves the minimum risk for the bullfighter and the maximum respect for the bull's susceptibilities in that it is not killed in public but in private. The first part of a Portuguese bullfight or *tourada* is conducted artistically and with great skill by a *cavaleiro* or horseman. He is dressed *á antiga Portuguesa* – 18th-century velvet suit embroidered in gold, tricorn hat, highly-polished black kneeboots. By his superb horsemanship he evades the bull's charges (though there is no risk of goring because the bull's horns are *embolados* or padded) and manages to jab a series of barbed *banderilhas* or *fardas* into the muscle around the bull's shoulder blades. These *banderilhas* dangle there and draw plenty of blood. When in due course the half-ton bull has been sufficiently weakened, eight agile young men called *moços de forcado* enter the ring and proceed to dominate the bull on foot in what develops into something very much like all-in wrestling – pulling the tail, grabbing the horns, jumping on the bull's back and being thrown off again. This phase is known as the *pega*. Something similar, according to Pliny, used to take place in Rome at the time of Julius Caesar. When the bull has had enough and stops resisting, it is freed and encouraged to follow a team of docile oxen with tinkling bells out of the ring. Then in comes the next bull. There are usually eight altogether on the day's programme.

As distinct from this normal sort of bullfight, many places (see regional introductions) 'run the bulls through the streets'. This is the less-organized but nevertheless exciting passage of the bulls through the barricaded streets on their way to the bullring for a later more formal appearance. Youths display their valour – or lack of it – in their efforts to separate one of the bulls from its companions and to play it with makeshift capes. You can watch the very brief proceedings from the safety of a barricaded side-street.

There are 33 bullrings (*praças de touros* or *toiros*) in Portugal and the season runs approximately from April to October. In the smaller towns bullfights are infrequent – two or three a year – usually during the annual *festa*. In Lisbon, in the ornate 19th-century *Campo Pequeño*, there are about 20, mostly on a Thursday afternoon. Santarém and Vila Franca de Xira, which are the two main centres of bull breeding, also stage bullfights fairly frequently. Tickets can be obtained at the bullring itself (it is advisable to buy them the day before at the height of the season) or from hotel porters (who will naturally charge you a little more). Seats in the sun are cheaper than those in the shade. There is no need to be on or even near the expensive front row. The seats are steeply banked and you get a far better panoramic view from about half-way back.

**Casinos** Although Portugal's casinos are all sited along the coast, and therefore mainly intended for summer visitors, they nevertheless stay open all the year round, except for Good Friday and Christmas Eve. There are seven of them: Espinho and Póvoa de Varzim (Costa Verde), Figueiro da Foz (Costa de Prata), Estoril (Lisbon) and Alvor, Vilamoura, and Monte Gordo (Algarve). Their hours of opening are standardized (1500–0300) and, apart from the gaming rooms, they all

have a restaurant and a nightly floor show. Some of them have shops and a cinema too. They all charge an entrance fee and foreign visitors must produce their passport. The most elegant and famous of them all – and indeed one of the most famous in the world – is that of Estoril, which publishes a folder (in Portuguese and English) for those who are visiting a casino for the first time. Men are requested to wear jackets and ties, at any rate after 2000 hrs. If you would like a table for the floor show (normally starting just before midnight) it is advisable to ask the hotel porter to make a prior reservation, or do it yourself.

**Cinema, theatre** Most of the films in the cinemas embody the original sound-track with printed sub-titles in Portuguese. The language barrier is thus removed for English-speaking visitors, and they can see and enjoy American and English films just as easily as they can at home. There are usually two sessions – at 1500 hrs and 2130 hrs. Similarly there is no language difficulty with opera, ballet, or music, all of which, however, are staged in the non-summer months and usually in the main towns, especially Lisbon and Porto. But there are summer shows in the open air and the local tourist information office always has details. Theatre shows – mostly comedies and revues – pose the language problem but can still be entertaining.

**Discothéques, nightclubs** There are discothéques everywhere, at every place on the coast and even at quite small places inland. They stay open until the early hours of the morning. Nightclubs often belong to the bigger hotels and you can alternately dance and watch the floor show. But casinos (see above) have raised the standard of entertainment and frequently offer lavishly-staged shows of international quality.

**Fado** Another form of entertainment – and the one that is most typically Portuguese – is *fado* singing, and the best place to hear it is in a so-called *fado* restaurant, where you are serenaded while you eat. The artists are the *fadista* or singer, usually a woman, usually dressed in black, and one or two accompanists playing 12-stringed Portuguese guitars. Together they extract the last grains of melancholy from the monotonous lament of thwarted love or passion or of a yearning for things that are not to be. The *fado*, some say, originated in the Congo, reached Portugal via African slaves in Brazil and became the signature tune of friendly young ladies in the lower haunts of Lisbon. But others say it was the medieval troubadours who popularized it and the beaux of the last century who developed it. There are *fado* restaurants all over Portugal but the best are in Lisbon, more especially in the Alfama, Bairro Alto and Mouraria districts. In the high season it is best to reserve a table in advance.

**Football** (soccer) The Portuguese share the world-wide enthusiasm for football. Every town and village has its team but the rival Lisbon teams of Benfica and Sporting are internationally famous, as is F.C. de Porto. Matches are played on Sundays and holidays, in the afternoon.

# WHAT YOU NEED TO KNOW

**Church** (Services in English, times liable to alteration) **Lisbon**: Baptist Evangelical Church, Rua F. Folque 36B, Sun. 1000 and 2130, Wed. 0930. Church of England, St George's Church, Rua da Estrela 4, Sun. 0830 and 1100. Church of Scotland, St Andrew's Church, Rua Arriaga 13, Sun. 1100. English College, Rua dos Inglesinhos, Sun. 0700 and 1000, Wed. 0700. Irish Dominican Church, Largo do Corpo Santo, Sun. 0700, 0800, 0900 and 1100, Wed. 0700, 0800 and 0900. Jewish Synagogue, Rua Alexandre Herculano 59, every day 0800 and at dusk. Presbyterian Evangelical Church, Rua T. Anunciação 36, Sun. 1000. **Carcavelos**: Parish Church, Largo da República, Roman Catholic mass in English every Sun. and holy day 1045. **Cascais**: Capela de São Sebastião, Parque Castro Guimarães, Roman Catholic mass in English, Sat. and eves of holy days 1830, Sun. 1200. Church of Jesus Christ of Latter-Day Saints (Mormon), Rua Ten. Coronel José Barros Pessoa 19, various meetings Sun. morning. 'American Fireside Group' 1st Sun. evening in month. **Estoril**: St Paul's Anglican Church, Avenida Bombeiros Voluntarios 1C, Sun. 0815 (holy communion), 1100 (morning prayer and sermon), 1200 (holy communion) 1st and 3rd Sun. **Porto**: British Church of St James (Anglican), Largo de Maternidade de Júlio Dinis, Sun. 0930 and 1000 and religious holidays.

**Cigarettes and Tobacco** Portuguese cigarettes (*cigarros*), cigars (*charutos*) and tobacco (*tabaco*) are sold at *tabacarias*. You might like to try such brands as SG, Porto or Ritz. American and British brands are plentiful in all tourist areas but cost three times as much as the local varieties.

**Correspondence** may be addressed to you c/o *Posta Restante* at the post office (*correio*) of any town you may be visiting.

**Electricity** Almost everywhere the voltage is 220 though there are a few places where it is 110. In most hotels there are shaving points which take the UK two-pin plug as well as the continental plug which is wider. To be absolutely safe it is advisable to buy an adaptor before leaving home. Shavers fitted with the American flat-pin plug also require an adaptor.

**Festivals and public holidays** Each town holds its own annual *festa* or festival. You will find brief details of some of them in the introductions to the six holiday regions. Very many places celebrate the night of 23–24 June (São João or St John) and the night of 28–29 June (São Pedro or St Peter) with street bonfires which young people jump through. Apart from these local festivals, there are 12 national holidays when all shops, banks and other businesses are closed, though bars, restaurants, public transport and most entertainments (except casinos on Good Friday and Christmas Eve) are not affected. Two of the *festas* have movable dates – Good Friday and Corpus Christi. The rest are: January 1 (the traditional revelries the night before including the eating of 12 grapes on the strokes of midnight to ensure 12 happy months); April 25, commemorating the *coup d'état* in 1974; May 1, Labour Day; June 10, commemorating Portugal's great writer, Luis de Camoens; August 15, bodily assumption of the Virgin Mary; October 5, Republic Day, celebrating the overthrow of the monarchy in 1910; November 1, All Saints' Day; December 1, Restauração (ending of 60 years of Spanish rule, 1640); December 8, Immaculate Conception; December 25, Christmas Day.

**Guides and interpreters** are available everywhere. They can be engaged through travel agencies or, sometimes, by hotel porters. The professional body of guide-interpreters (Rua do Telhal 4,3o, Lisbon, or Rua Nova de Avilha, Porto, or Avenida Marnoco e Sousa 35-r/c dto., Coimbra, or Rua do Letes 32, Faro) can be approached direct by groups or individuals.

**Hairdressers** for men are called *barbeiros* and for women *cabeleireiros*. A permanent wave is *uma permanente*, a shampoo and set *lavar e mise*, a haircut *cortar el pelo*, a shave *fazer a barba*. (See Tipping p. 24.)

**Health** Chemists' shops (*farmácias*) can usually prescribe for minor ailments or put you in touch with a doctor for more serious matters. There is always one chemist's shop open day and night on a rota basis in every small town and in every district of big towns. Hall porters, tourist information offices, and police stations will direct you to the *farmácia do turno* or duty chemist. You will find the address, however, displayed in the windows of all closed chemists' shops and it also appears each day in the press. **Local hospitals** are usually open 24 hours a day and will give emergency assistance or advice. In Lisbon the **British Hospital** (address: Rua Saraiva Carvalho 49, tel. 602020) holds an outpatients' clinic every day 1030–1300 and 1800–2000 and has English-speaking staff. (See insurance, p. 10.)

**Lost property** Most Portuguese (and, one hopes, most fellow guests) are honest. But, as in any other country, take precautions. Close bedroom windows if access is possible from an adjoining balcony. Never leave money, valuables, passports, or return tickets in an hotel bedroom, apartment, motor car, or caravan. Also, keep your hand on your wallet in crowded places and carry your handbag out of snatching reach of delinquents on motor cycles. If you are robbed or otherwise lose anything report it immediately to the police (*Polícia de Segurança Pública*). It is most important to obtain a written statement from them that you have done so, for many insurance companies make this a condition for accepting your claim. If you are travelling with a group, the tour operator's representative should also be informed. In Lisbon there is a lost property office at Rua dos Anjos 56A (tel. 366141).

**Newspapers and magazines** British newspapers (at rather more than double their published price) generally arrive in the tourist resorts and main cities the day of publication or the day after. So does the Paris edition of the *Herald Tribune*, published jointly by the *Washington Post* and the *New York Times*. Some American and British magazines and English language books are also available.

**Opening times** Shops in non-tourist areas open 0900–1300 and 1500–1900 Monday–Friday and 0900–1300 Saturday. In tourist areas they stay open as long as there is a prospect of custom, and open on Sundays too. **Banks.** See Currency, p. 12. **Post Offices** (*Correio*) are normally open 0900–1900 Monday–Friday but some close at 1800 and some 1230–1400. In Lisbon the post office in Praça dos Restauradores is open 0800–2400, also in Porto that in Praça General Humberto Delgado, and the telephone and telegraph offices in the same buildings. **Cafés and bars** – all day long except for approx. 2400–0800. **Museums** open every day 1000–1700 except Monday and festivals. Some stay open later and some (*eg* those at Queluz) close Tuesday instead of Monday. It is advisable to check with a tourist office before visiting. At all museums there is an entrance fee except on Sunday. **Frontier posts** Only a few of Portugal's 13 frontier posts – all with Spain – remain open 24 hours a day and even these only at Easter, Christmas and 1 July–30 Sept. As there is no uniformity of opening hours it is essential to check before arriving. You are quite safe, however, if you arrive at any of the posts 0800–1800.

**Public conveniences** (in Portuguese *lavabos, toilettes* or *retretes*) are reasonably plentiful in the main towns and tourist resorts but scarce or non-existent elsewhere. One is thus dependent upon those in cafés and bars. They are marked *homens* (men) and *senhoras* (women) or have some self-evident symbol such as a figure in skirt or trousers.

**Radio and TV**. The BBC World Service, broadcasting 24 hours a day, gives frequent news bulletins apart from other programmes. A short-wave receiver is essential, the best wavelengths for Portugal being 19.91m, 24.80m and 31.88m according to the time of day. Reception of US stations is generally poor. The Portuguese radio broadcasts breakfast-time English language programmes of interest to visitors. On Portuguese TV (black and white and colour) there are often British and American films with original soundtracks and Portuguese subtitles.

**Shopping** The most enterprising of the supermarkets in the tourist areas – especially in the Algarve – are well stocked with foods imported from Britain and North America. But everywhere you will find interesting things. Best buys to take home are *Serra da Estrela* cheese, *broa* (a maize bread which keeps well, best known in the northern half of the country), port and other wines, olive oil, all kinds of clothes especially heavy-knit sweaters, articles of wood, cork, leather, copper, and filigree jewellery, hand-painted tiles, hand-embroidered table cloths and bedspreads. And perhaps a small 'Barcelos cock' (see p. 25) or a cassette of *fado* music sung by the famous Amália Rodrigues ('Amália Fado')? By the way, you can bargain, if you like, at market stalls but not of course in shops.

**Telephone** Calls can be made from any main post office, some of whom have English-speaking staff who will handle the call for you and collect its cost afterwards. Or you can dial direct from a public telephone booth. Dialling code is 00 for *internacional* followed by 44 for UK, 353 for Eire, 1 for USA and Canada, 61 for Australia, 64 for New Zealand, 27 for South Africa, and then the required number. Alternatively calls may be made by the hotel receptionist and taken in your room but for this service there is naturally an additional charge. For **telegrams** see Opening Times p. 23.

**Time** Portuguese time is the same as UK time, *ie* in winter Greenwich Mean Time and in summer one hour ahead of it. In summer New York and Montreal are five hours behind Portuguese time and Los Angeles eight hours behind. Cape Town is one hour ahead of Portuguese time and Sydney 10 hours ahead.

**Tipping** Although a service charge is included in hotel, restaurant, and café bills, it is still customary to tip. A reasonable amount would be eight or ten percent. This would be appropriate for hairdressers too. It is also customary to tip taxi drivers by perhaps slightly more than that. You could give hotel porters 10–20 escudos for helping you with your luggage and the same amount or less to cinema and theatre usherettes or bullfight attendants for showing you to your seat. Public lavatory attendants also expect a tip but this needn't be more than three to five escudos.

**Toilets** (See Public Conveniences).

**Tourist Information** is available by telephone in Lisbon in five languages with a special number for each. The English number is 369450 preceded by 01 if dialling from outside the Lisbon area. A similar service is available in Porto at (02-317514).

## Portuguese National Tourist Offices:

**Canada** 390 Bay St, Toronto, Ontario M5H 2Y2 (364 8133); Suite 1150, 1801 McGill College Ave, Montreal, Quebec H3A 2N4 (282 1264). **UK** 1–5 New Bond St, London W1 (493 3873). **US** 548 Fifth Ave, New York NY 10036 (954 4403); Suite 3001, 919 North Michigan Ave, Chicago IL 60611 (236 6603); Suite 616, 3440 Wilshire Bvd, Los Angeles CA 90010 (380 6459).

## Embassies (e), Consulates (c)

**Australia (e)** Avenida da Liberdade 244, Lisbon (539108). **Canada (e)** Rua Rosa Araújo 2, Lisbon (562547). **Eire (e)** Rua da Imprensa à Estrela 1, Lisbon (661569). **South Africa (e)** Avenida Luís Bívar 10, Lisbon (535041). **UK (e)** Rua São Domingos à Lapa 35–37, Lisbon (661191, 661122, 661147, 663181). **(c)** Avenida da Boavista 3072, Porto (684789); **(c)** Rua Santa Isabel 21, Portimão (Algarve) (23071); **(c)** Rua General Humberto Delgado 4, Vila Real de Santo Antonio (Algarve) (43729). **US (e)** Avenida Duque de Loulé 39, Lisbon (570102, 570627). **(c)** Rua Julio Dinis 826, Porto (63094).

# LANGUAGE

The Portuguese language derives from the corrupt Latin spoken by the inhabitants of the Iberian Peninsula when the Roman domination ended in ADc414 Resisting the influence of Castilian which gradually developed in neighbouring Spain, it became a literary language in the 13th century and received tremendous stimulus from King Dinis (1279–1325) who himself wrote poems and pastorals that have seldom been excelled. It is a difficult language to learn. It resembles Spanish when written but hardly at all when spoken. Fortunately for Anglo-Saxon visitors it is always possible to find someone in shops, banks, restaurants and anywhere else who speaks English. Nevertheless most people find themselves picking up a few words and phrases to prove to their hosts that they are at least willing.

| | |
|---|---|
| Good morning | *Bom dia* (bon dee´ă) |
| Good afternoon | *Boa tarde* (boh´ă tard) |
| Good night | *Boa noite* (boh´ă noheet) |
| Please | *Faz favor* (fash fǎ-vohr´) |
| Thank you | *Obrigado* (or if you are a woman) *obrigada* (oh-bree-gah´doo/oh-bree-gah´dă) |
| Yes/no | *Sim/não* (seen/nown) |
| How much? | *Quanto custa?* (Kwan´too koosh-´tǎ) |
| Excuse me | *Perdão* (per-down´) |
| Not at all | *De nada* (dě nah´dǎ) |
| Goodbye | *Adeus* (ǎ-day´oosh) |

The pronunciation is difficult and the guide is only an approximation. The emphasis is on the syllable preceding the ´. A nasal sound precedes the italic *n*. The vowels marked ǎ, ě are pronounced as in *above, sofa* and *open,* spoken. It is a help to take with you Collins *Portuguese Phrase Book* and Collins *Portuguese–English Gem Dictionary*.

This is not a vocabulary list. It is merely a supplement to the words and names appearing on the maps and town plans.

| | |
|---|---|
| airport | *aeroporto* |
| bread shop | *padaria* |
| beach | *praia* |
| bookshop | *livraria* |
| bridge | *ponte* |
| bus station | *estação de autocarros* |
| butcher's | *talho* |
| cake shop | *pastelaria* |
| camp site | *parque de campismo* |
| casino | *casino* |
| castle | *castelo* |
| cathedral | *sé* |

| | | | |
|---|---|---|---|
| chapel | *capela* | petrol/gasoline | *gasolina* |
| chemist's | *farmácia* | petrol/gas station | *posto da gasolina* |
| church | *igreja* | police station | *posto da polícia* |
| convent | *convento* | post office | *correio* |
| farm | *quinta* | quay | *cais* |
| ferry | *ferry* | railway station | *estação de caminho* |
| fish shop | *peixaria* | | *de ferro* |
| fountain | *fonte* | spa | *estância termal* |
| garage | *garagem* | square | *praça* |
| garden | *jardim* | supermarket | *supermercado* |
| greengrocer's | *hortaliceiro* | swimming pool | *piscina* |
| hospital | *hospital* | telephone | *telefone* |
| house | *casa* | telephone kiosk | *cabina telefónica* |
| inn | *estalagem* | theatre | *teatro* |
| library | *biblioteca* | tobacconist's shop | *tabacaria* |
| market | *mercado* | tourist | *posto de turismo* |
| monastery | *mosteiro* | information | |
| museum | *museu* | town centre | *centro cidade* |
| palace | *palácio* or *paço* | town hall | *câmara municipal* |
| park | *parque* | university | *universidade* |

*top l, Arrábida, top r; Mending nets, btm l; Barcelos cockerels, btm r; River Lima*

# COSTA VERDE

This most northerly of Portugal's six holiday regions is perhaps the loveliest. It is green because of one thing – rain. While the summers are hot and ideal for bathing – it has 150km/93mi of mostly sandy beaches – the winters are long, always warm but usually wet. The region has three rivers – the Minho (which separates it from Spain), the Lima and the Douro – and three administrative districts: Viana do Castelo, Braga and Porto. Historically it was the original Portugal – the county of Portucale which the king of neighbouring Castile and León gave to Count Henry of Burgundy in 1095 in gratitude for his help in driving out the Moors. Count Henry's son Afonso became Portugal's first king.

Today it is a fertile agricultural region where the tractor has not yet completely ousted the ox with its elaborately-carved yoke and screeching, wooden-axled cart. This region is the home of *vinho verde*, the young, slightly fizzy wine made from grapes whose vines grow over pergolas or are sometimes trained high up into trees. It is also the home of port (see p. 18), an industry the British have largely controlled since the wool-for-wine agreement of 1703.

**Festivals** Holy Week: Braga – biggest religious processions in Portugal. March (3rd week): Póvoa de Lanhoso (Braga) – St Joseph's festival with folk dancing, horse race, fireworks. May (1st week): Barcelos – ceramics fair and folk dancing. June (1st Sat.): Amarante – *festa* of St Gonçalo. June 29: Póvoa de Varzim – torchlight procession, sardine barbecue. Aug. (1st week): Guimarães – 'procession of the saints', bands, folk dancing, singing, fireworks. Aug. 15: Póvoa de Varzim – blessing of fishing boats. Aug. (two days preceding last Sunday): Viana do Castelo – one of the biggest popular *festas* in country. Sept. (3rd week): Ponte de Lima (Viana do Castelo) – *feiras novas* ('new fairs', though they date back to 12th century), buy–sell–or–exchange for farmers, procession, folklore, bullfight, fireworks over river.

## Amarante                                          F7

*Porto* (pop. 4000) A small wine-making town divided in two by the River Tâmega. It still has many fine 16th–18th-century houses with quaint wooden balconies. Some of them are perched in tiers above the river and, from the opposite bank, with the **Convent of St Gonçalo** (built 1540–1620) in the background and the three-arched obelisked bridge (1781–90)

below, provide one of the loveliest architectural views in Portugal. The convent itself contains the tomb of St Gonçalo who died c1259 and is the patron saint of marriages, an accolade for which he seems to have qualified by living a celibate life in a hermitage. Unmarried men believe that by rubbing his tombstone with their bare flesh they will acquire a wife within a year. On the 1st Sat. June, in the saint's honour, local shops sell cakes in the form of a phallus, which young couples present to each other in great glee and without noticeable embarrassment. The town hall exhibits paintings by Amadeu de Sousa Cardoso who was a friend of Modigliani and sat for *The Portuguese* by Braque. *Braga 55km/34mi.*

## Barcelos                                          E4

*Braga* (pop. 5500) This is an attractive agricultural market town (market Thursday and one of the most interesting in Portugal) noted for its handicrafts – embroidery, handwoven textiles, carved horse and oxen yokes, baskets and straw hats. But its best-known industry is brightly-coloured pottery, especially the 'Barcelos cock', which has almost become the national symbol of Portugal and which saved the life of a pilgrim sentenced to be hanged for theft. The pilgrim called upon the already-roasted cock, destined for the judge's dinner, to testify to his innocence by crowing, which it did. A monument to the miracle (erected by the very shaken judge himself) is now in the open-air archaeological museum in the ruins of the 15th-century **Palace of the Dukes of Bragança.** The palace basement houses a ceramics museum. See also the **parish church** (*igreja matriz*) which has a Romanesque doorway and tiled walls. In the river beneath the much-restored bridge lampreys are reared for market. *Braga 17km/11mi.*

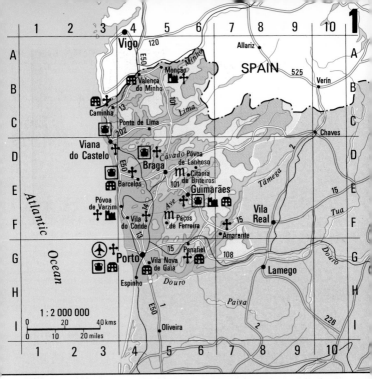

| | 1 | 2 | 3 | 4 | 5 | 6 | 7 | 8 | 9 | 10 |
|---|---|---|---|---|---|---|---|---|---|---|

Vigo 120

Allariz

SPAIN 525

Verín

A

Mençión

Valença do Minho

B

Caminha

Ponte de Lima

13

Lima

Minho

101

C

Chaves

202

Viana do Castelo

D

Braga

Cávado

Póvoa de Lanhoso

Citânia de Briteiros

Tâmega

E50

Barcelos

101

E

Póvoa de Varzim

Guimarães

Ave

Vila Real

15

Tua

Vila do Conde

Paços de Ferreira

Amarante

15

Douro

F

Atlantic

Porto

15

Penafiel

108

G

Ocean

Vila Nova de Gaia

Lamego

Espinho

Douro

H

E50

Paiva

I

1 : 2 000 000

Oliveira

226

0    20    40 kms
0   10   20 miles

*Amarante*

## Braga                                    E5

*Braga* (pop. 40,000) This was an important Roman settlement before the birth of Christ and is today a rather sprawling industrial and agricultural market town making cutlery, jewellery, textiles, and soap. It is the seat of an archbishop. Almost all the numerous churches have granite façades and twin belfries. The **cathedral** was built in the 12th century, though all that has survived of the original Romanesque fabric is the south portal and part of the main doorway. Among its great treasures are Portugal's earliest known murals, dating from 1330. For a fee one can also visit the **Museum of Sacred Art**, the **Chapel of São Geraldo** (St Gerard, first archbishop of Braga) containing the 12th-century tombs of Henry of Burgundy and his wife Teresa, parents of Portugal's first king, Afonso I, and the mummified body of Archbishop Lourenço Vicente; the **Kings' Chapel** (*Capela dos Reis*) and the **Chapel of Glory** (*Capela da Glória*) containing the 16th-century profusely-carved tomb of Bishop Gonçalo Pereira. See also in Braga: the **Old Episcopal Palace** (*Antigo Paço Episcopal*), 14th–18th-century, containing one of the most valuable libraries in Portugal (10,000 MSS, 300,000 books) and the 16th-century **Chapel of the Dukes of Coimbra** (*Capela dos Coimbras*) with tiled interior. 6km/4mi east of Braga the pilgrimage church of **Bom Jesus do Monte** stands on a wooded hill. Approach is by the car road, on foot up the winding way of the cross lined with 18th-century octagonal chapels, by an impressive monumental staircase lined with fountains (some pilgrims climb it on their knees) or by funicular railway. Beyond Bom Jesus, 4km/2.5mi, is **Monte Sameiro** crowned by a modern church from the top of whose tower (reached by a spiral staircase of 250 steps) there is a breathtaking panoramic view. 10km/6mi still further from Braga are the ruins of **Citânia de Briteiros**, an Iron Age city of 150 stone habitations (two of which have been reconstructed) protected by perimeter walls. Many of the objects found here are in the Museum of Martins Sarmento in Guimarães. (See Guimarães).

## Caminha                                  C3

*Viana do Castelo* (pop. 1500) Caminha stands picturesquely at the mouth of the River Minho guarding the frontier with Spain. It still has its fortifications but is today a peaceful fishing village. In the medieval-looking main square are several fine 15th-century houses, the town hall, a 16th-century granite fountain, the Gothic

Palace of the Pictas and a 15th-century clock tower. The fortified parish church (*igreja matriz*), designed by Spanish architects in 1490, has many interesting features including a very lovely wooden ceiling carved by Francisco Munoz in 1565. *Porto 91km/56mi.*

## Espinho                                  H4

*Viseu* (pop. 15,000) is a modern holiday resort. It has a casino, an 18-hole golf course, streets that are numbered instead of named, and makes painted furniture. *Porto 16km/10mi.*

## Guimarães                                E6

*Braga* (pop. 25,000) This was Portugal's first capital, birthplace of Portugal's first king (Afonso Henriques, 1128–85), of the playright Gil Vicente (c1465–c1536) and of Pope Damasus, 366–84. The **Church of St Francis** (*Igreja São Francisco*), built 14th century and remodelled 17th, has 16th-century cloisters and a nave covered with *azulejos* depicting St Francis of Assisi preaching to the fishes. The Church of Our Lady of the Olive Tree (*Igreja Nossa Senhora da Oliveira*) was so-named, it is said, because the Visigoth chief Wamba, on being informed by a messenger in 672 that the royal council had elected him king, and having no wish for the crown, declared that he would accept if the olive staff he was carrying sprouted leaves, which it immediately did. The legend is more specifically commemorated by the small shrine (built 1342) outside the church. Part of this church, including the lovely 13th-century cloister, houses the **Alberto Sampaio Museum** containing many objects of interest including a door from the 10th-century monastery of Princess Mumadona, who was virtual founder of the town, statuary, altar-pieces, paintings, ceramics, tiles and the valuable church treasures. The Palace of the Dukes of Bragança (*Paço dos Duques*) is a 15th-century building abandoned in the 16th, used as a barracks until 1935 and more recently inappropriately given a mansard roof in pink tiles. Today it is a museum of tapestries, carpets, furniture, porcelain, and paintings. The **Martins Sarmento Museum**, installed in the lovely cloister of the Church of São Domingos, contains many of the objects discovered in 1875 at the Celtiberian site Citânia de Briteiros (see Braga, above) by the archaeologist after whom the museum is named. Among the exhibits is the awesome Colossus of Pedralua – a 3m/10ft high seated granite figure. The 12th-century nine-towered castle which crowns the hill above the town has a massive 27m/88ft high keep and in the 19th century was used as a debtors' prison. *Braga 22km/13mi.*

## Monção A5

*Viana do Castelo* (pop. 3000) An attractive walled town overlooking the River Minho which forms the boundary with Spain. Its 12th-century castle has a history of sieges. In one of them, in 1368, a local heroine, Deu-la-Deu Martins, used the subterfuge of throwing loaves of bread to the bésiegers to show them the futility of demanding surrender. There is a monument to her in the main square and her tomb is in the lovely Romanesque church. Another siege, in 1658, lasted four months but this time the defenders were starving, and surrendered. The town is noted for its wine, *vinho verde*, its medicinal waters and the delicious lampreys which spawn in the River Minho. *Braga 78km/48mi.*

## Penafiel G6

*Porto* (pop. 6000) A town of no great attraction except for its old granite houses, many with gargoyles and iron grilles. In the Rua Direita, numbers 82 and 126 (an elegant 18th-century palace) are particularly interesting. See also the Church of the Misericórdia with its tiled cupola and unique screen surmounting the 'board'

pew. *Porto 35km/22mi.* Beyond the village of Paços de Ferreira, 14km/9mi northwest, is the important Iron Age settlement **Citânia de Sanfins**, with 150 stone dwellings, some of them restored.

## Porto (Oporto) G4

*Porto* (pop. 350,000, Greater Porto 750,000) Portugal's second largest city is world-famous for its port wine but has other valuable industries including textiles, tyres, chemicals, leather, ceramics, fishing, canning, and filigree work in gold and silver. It stands on the rocky north bank of the River Douro with the daughter-town of Vila Nova de Gaia, where most of the *armazens* or wine warehouses are situated, on the opposite side. Three bridges cross the river: the railway bridge (1877) designed by the famous French engineer Gustave Eiffel, the road bridge (1886) designed by Eiffel's pupil Theophilus Seyrig, and the motorway bridge (1963) which is said to contain the biggest concrete arch in the world, designed by the Portuguese engineer Edgar Cardoso. Porto has two ports, one, like the city itself, 5km/3mi from the sea, the other, a seaport, at Leixões 10km/6mi to the north. Porto's inhabitants have long been known as the *tripeiros* or tripe-eaters,

*Two views of Porto from Vila Nova de Gaia*

a nickname that originated in 1415 when King João I victualled his fleet with the best meat for his expedition to capture Ceuta (the first of Portugal's African colonies) and left only the offal for the folks at home. Tripe, cooked with dried beans, is still the traditional local dish. It was here in 1809, during the Peninsular War, that Wellington's troops crossed the river in four discarded wine barges and he himself sat down to the lavish lunch left untasted by the hastily departing French marshall, Soult. (But hundreds of the inhabitants, rushing across the 'bridge of boats' before Soult destroyed it, had been drowned and there is a monument recalling the disaster near the road bridge).

Standing high above a maze of narrow streets that wind up from the harbour (**Rua Cimo da Vila** is an especially fascinating example) is the twin-towered **cathedral**, built and fortified in the 12th century but drastically altered in the 17th and 18th, still, however, having traces of the original Romanesque, including a doorway, a lovely rose window and part of the cloister. Worth seeing are the 17th-century holy water stoop, the altar with 17th-century silver altarpiece supplied by nine different silversmiths and a bronze relief by Teixeira Lopes depicting the baptism of Christ. In the cathedral in 1387 João I married Philippa of Lancaster, daughter of John of Gaunt.

Among the city's churches see that of **São Francisco**, 17th-century with a wealth of gilded wood carving and original rose window; **dos Clérigos**, built 1748–63 by the Italian architect Nicolas Nassoni and having the highest tower (10-storey, 75m/246ft) in Portugal whose 240 steps can be ascended by those wishing to see the tremendous view from the top. Among the numerous museums (fuller details obtainable the tourist office: Praça Dom João I 43): **Soares dos Reis** housed in the 18th-century Carrancas Palace (pottery, Portuguese primitives, 19th- and 20th-century paintings, religious art, jewellery) and **Guerra Junqueiro** (art objects collected by the satirical poet (1850–1923) of this name).

The wine warehouses on the south side of the river, in Vila Nova de Gaia, may be visited and the wine tasted.

## Póvoa de Varzim                     F4

*Porto* (pop. 25,000) This is an old fishing port whose long sandy beach has enabled it to develop into a modern holiday resort. In the picturesque fishing quarter fisherwomen mend nets and help in the collection of seaweed that is then dried in the sun and sold as fertilizer. There are the ruins of an 18th-century fortress and a small folklore museum. Carpets, colourful embroidery and woollen jerseys are made locally. The town was the birthplace of the novelist José Maria Eça de Queirós (1845–1900) who served as the Portuguese Consul while living in Britain. *Porto 31km/19mi.*

*Selling octopus in Póvoa do Varzim*

## Valença do Minho                 B4

*Viana do Castelo* (pop. 2000) A frontier town, part old, part modern. The old town, completely enclosed by a well-preserved 17th-century wall, faces the Spanish town of Túy across the lovely Minho river. *Braga 61km/38mi.*

## Viana do Castelo                 D3

*Viana do Castelo* (pop. 16,000) Standing at the mouth of the river Lima (whose gentle flow earned it the name of the river of forgetfulness) this is a pleasant holiday resort with a fleet of boats that fish for cod off Newfoundland. It also has a naval shipyard. It is noted for textiles, ceramics, and filigree work. See: the parish church (*igreja matriz*), mainly 14th–15th-century but the towers flanking the west door are Romanesque; the **Church of the Misericórdia** facing the triangular Praça de la República (in the centre of which is an elegant 16th-century fountain) has an impressive façade formed by superimposed loggias; the **municipal museum,** housed in the 18th-century palace of the Barbosa Macieis family and containing furniture, ceramics, paintings, and *azulejos.* For a good view of the town and surroundings, drive (or take the funicular) to the hill of Santa Luzia (200m/656ft). *Porto 67km/41mi.*

## Vila do Conde                 F4

*Porto* (pop. 18,000) This combined holiday resort and fishing port has shipyards, cotton mills, and a chocolate factory and is also famous for its lace. It stands at the mouth of the River Ave. Above it is the huge **Convent of Santa Clara**, the 16th-century church of which contains the ornate tombs of the founder, Afonso Sanches (illegitimate son of King Dinis) and his wife, and other notables. In the cloister is a fountain fed by the partly ruined aqueduct (built 1705–14, 999 arches, 5km/3mi long). See also the parish church (*igreja matriz*) and, facing it, the 18th-century pillory surmounted by the sword of justice. *Porto 27km/17mi.*

*Seaweed gatherer, Apúlia*

*Local costume, Viana do Casteló*

# COSTA DE PRATA

This region comprises the administrative districts of Aveiro, Coimbra, and Leiria and part of that of Lisbon. It has a coastline measuring 280km/173 miles, for the most part sandy with innumerable beaches, though north of Nazaré and south of Peniche it is rocky. There are many attractive lagoons, estuaries, and sheltered inlets. It is not difficult for you to enjoy secluded bathing but also to be more sociable in the evenings, if you wish, at nightclubs, discotheques or casinos. In this region some of Portugal's best wine is produced – the sparkling and still wines of Bairrada and the somewhat stronger vintages of Alcobaça, Caldas and Óbidos (noted also for its cherry brandy called *ginginha*). Traditional dishes that you might like to try are (on the coast) fried eels (*enguias fritas*) and mussels on the spit (*espetadas de mexilhões*) or (inland) casserole of lamb (*carneiro na caçoila preta*) and the delicious roast suckling pig (*leitão*).

The historic battle of Aljubarrota (1385) was fought here between the armies of two contenders for the Portuguese throne. (See Batalha.) It was here too that the Portuguese and British armies under Wellington fought some of the great but costly battles of the Peninsular War against Napoleon – at Roliça, Vimeiro and Buçaco (see p. 36).

**Festivals** Jan. 20: Vila da Feira (Aveiro) – festival of St Sebastian; procession of little girls carrying *fogaças* (buns, flowers, ribbons) on their heads. Feb.–March (three days before Ash Wednesday): Ovar (Aveiro) and Nazaré (Leiria) – *carnaval* (revelry). May–Oct. (12–13 each month): Fátima (Leiria) – anniversaries of Virgin's six appearances in 1917. Aug.: Batalha (Leiria) – *Festa* of Our Lady of the Victory. Aug.: Aveiro – marine festival and decorated fishing boats competition. Aug. (1st week): Peniche (Leiria) – fishermen's festival of Our Lady of the Good Voyage: processions, grilled sardines for all, fireworks over sea. Sept. 7–15: Nazaré (Leiria) – festival of Our Lady of Nazaré (Nazareth); three days of processions followed by three days of dancing, folk singing, fireworks, bullfights.

## Alcobaça                                    L5

*Leiria* (pop. 5000) Standing at the confluence of the rivers Alcoa and Baça, Alcobaça is noted for its fruit and wine. It is a small, attractive town with an enormous **monastery** built by Cistercian monks on land presented to them in 1147

by Afonso I in thanksgiving for his victory over the Moors at Santarém. The monastery has the largest church in Portugal. The enormous length (109m/358ft) is nearly five times its width. Two rows of 13 columns support the 20m/66ft high roof and accentuate the Romanesque simplicity. In the **King's Hall** (*Sala dos Reis*) to the left of the entrance (but access from cloister) are life-size portraits of Portuguese kings and a capacious cauldron used for making soup for Spanish troops before it was captured by the Portuguese at the great battle of Aljubarrota (see Batalha) in 1385. The monks of the monastery also clearly liked their food – see the huge, lofty kitchen with its great open fireplaces, big enough to roast six oxen at a time. The kitchen has running water diverted from a stream. Next to the kitchen is the vaulted refectory. The 'cloister of silence' is 14th-century and the upper storey 16th. Stairs lead to the monks' dormitory.

But what most captures the popular imagination are the tombs of the royal lovers, Pedro I (1357–67) and Inês de Castro. The young Prince Pedro, married in 1336 to Constanza of Castile, falls in love with the beautiful Inês, one of his wife's ladies-in-waiting, whom he installs in a convent in Coimbra, where she bears him several children. When in 1345 his wife dies in childbirth he marries Inês secretly, aware of the fierce antagonism of his father, the king. But three noblemen, encouraged by the king, murder Inês in cold blood on 7 January 1355. When, two years later, Pedro inherits the throne he arrests two of the three murdering noblemen (the third escapes) and has them lengthily tortured and executed in his presence. He then has the body of Inês exhumed. Dressed in luxurious clothes, he seats her beside him on the throne with the royal crown on her head and

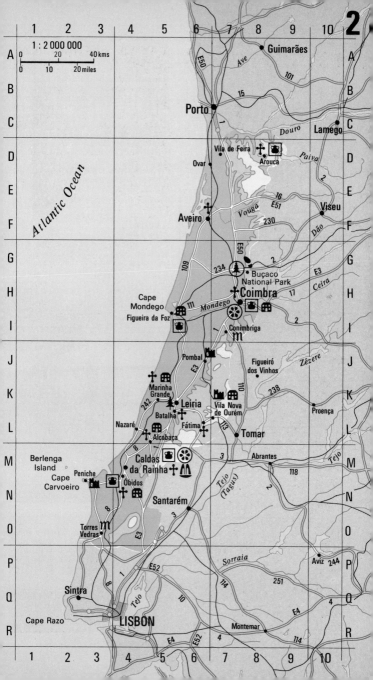

orders the nobility to file past and kiss the fleshless hand of the posthumously-crowned queen. Then, accompanied by a macabre torchlight procession, the body is carried 103km/65mi from Coimbra to Alcobaça and laid to rest in the huge tomb you can see in the chancel of the church today. On the other side of the chancel Pedro himself is buried, his tomb foot-to-foot with hers, so that, he said, the first sight his eyes would see on the day of resurrection will be the sweet face of his beloved Inês. On each tomb are the words 'until the end of the world'. *Leiria 32km/20mi.*

*Tomb of Inês de Castro*

## Arouca                                    D8

*Aveiro* (pop. 2000) This is just a small isolated village in a pleasant valley surrounded by wooded mountains. But it has the remains of a great **convent**, founded c710, destroyed by the Moors, rebuilt and ceded to the Cistercians soon after the order was founded in 1100. Its most famous abbess was Mafalda (c1194/1256), daughter of Sancho I, who was both queen (she was married at 21 to Enrique I of Castile, then aged 12) and posthumously saint. Her embalmed body, in glass and silver coffin, is in the convent church

(rebuilt 1704). There is a legend that the body was brought here strapped to the back of a mule which had been elected to arbitrate between the rival claims of Arouca and another Cistercian convent in Porto. Having been set free in neutral countryside, the mule made its way – 'reverently' it is said – to Arouca. See also in the church the carved choir stalls (1722–5), the larger-than-lifesize 18th-century statues of nuns (with rouged lips) and the small museum of sacred art on the upper floor of the cloister. During the Peninsular War (1808–14) Lt.-Gen. Sir William Warre, accompanied by Field-Marshal Beresford, visited the convent to see one of the nuns – his sister Clara. *Porto 76km/47mi.*

## Aveiro                                    F6

*Aveiro* (pop. 25,000) stands on the edge of a vast, irregular-shaped lagoon that is fed by three rivers, measures 36km/22mi from north to south, has an area of 6000 hectares/15,000 acres and only one narrow outlet to the sea. The lagoon is a universal provider – of fish, of salt by evaporation on its banks, of seaweed (for fertilizer) trawled from the bottom by picturesque boats called *moliceiros*, and of revenue from

*A moliceiro on the lagoon*

*Aviero*

*Batalha Monastery*

tourists who are taken for trips in boats. The town's other industries include ship-building, engineering, fish canning, rice growing, and the raising of cattle on the surrounding marshes, which are dotted with hump-backed bridges and wind-mills. The era of greatest prosperity for Aveiro was the mid-16th century when its boats fished the cod banks of Newfoundland. But in 1575 a tremendous storm built up huge banks of sand and completely blocked the town's access to the sea. Its port became useless and its trade was strangled. The population fell from 14,000 to 5000. All attempts to clear an outlet failed until in 1808 one succeeded and the prosperity of the town has since recovered.

The sightseer today should visit the regional museum housed in the 16th-century former **Convent of Jesus**. Among the many treasures are Portuguese primitives and an outstanding oil painting, attributed to Nuno Gonçalves (see p. 8), of Princess-Saint Joana who spent the last 18 years of her life here and is buried in the lower chancel.

## Batalha                                    L5

*Leiria* (pop. 7000). The name *batalha* or battle derives from the great battle of Aljubarrota in 1385 between João of Avis, recently proclaimed king, and a rival contender for the Portuguese throne, Juan I of Castile. The Castilian force numbered 30,000, mostly cavalry supported by powerful cannon. The 6,000 Portuguese, helped by a small force of English archers, were all on foot. It was clear to João of Avis that only a miracle could save him from annihilation. So he prayed to the

Virgin that she should perform such a miracle, promising that in gratitude he would build a great church to her glory. Next day, 14 August, at dawn, the battle began. In the first hour 2500 Spaniards were killed. The local population joined in. The baker's wife felled seven Spanish soldiers with the peel she normally used for her oven. (There is still a Portuguese saying: 'as full of fight as the baker's wife of Aljubarrota'). By the end of the day Juan of Castile had fled, leaving the Portuguese unexpectedly victorious – a victory that was to bring their country 200 years of peace.

The 'great church' that João built in fulfilment of his vow became the *Mosteiro de Batalha* (**Battle Abbey**) of which Huguet, an Irishman, was one of the designers. It is today among Portugal's foremost shrines and certainly one of her most elaborate medieval monuments. The west front, with its many pinnacles, has been likened to that of York Minster. It embodies a sculpture of Christ surrounded by saints. To the right of the entrance is the Founder's Chapel (*Capela do Fundador*) 20m/66ft square and containing the huge canopied combined tomb of João and his English queen Philippa of Lancaster, daughter of John of Gaunt. In the carving they are shown lying hand-in-hand. The tombs of four of their six brilliant sons, including Henrique (Henry the Navigator, 1394–1460) are also here. The chancel is lit with stained glass windows, rare in Portuguese churches. The lovely royal cloister (*claustro real*), measuring 50m/164ft by 55m/180ft, gives access to the beautifully-vaulted chapter house, containing the tombs of two unknown soldiers. The daring conception of the vaulting brought its designer Afonso Domingues so much criticism that, when the work was finished, he showed his confidence in its safety by spending the night beneath it. (In the building of it, however, he had employed convicts already condemned to death.) At the rear of the church, with a separate entrance through an outstandingly lovely doorway, are the seven unfinished chapels (*capelas imperfeitas*) radiating from a central octagon. They were planned by Duarte (1433–38), son of João of Avis, for his own mausoleum but he died before they were completed. *Leiria 11km/7mi.*

## Berlenga Island                    M2

*Leiria* This is the largest of a group of islands that lie 12km/7mi off Cape Carveiro. It is about a mile long, half a mile wide and rises 85m/279ft above the sea. It has a lighthouse, an old fort (now a youth hostel), which 28 Portuguese valiantly defended against 1500 Spaniards attacking from sailing ships in 1666, and the ruins of a monastery founded in 1513 but later abandoned as being too inaccessible. Between June and September there are boat services from Peniche (see p. 41) on the mainland (50 mins each way) and other boat trips from the island itself to smaller islands, some of which have marine tunnels of great beauty. A walk around the main island would also repay the more energetic. You may well see the wild black rabbit which inhabits this island.

## Buçaco National Park           H8

*Aveiro* This comprises 100 hectares/250 acres of well-cared-for woodland planted with 700 varieties of indigenous and foreign trees including the very rare Mexican cypress which sometimes reaches 35m/115ft in height and 5m/16ft in girth. For more than 1000 years the forest has been church property, providing a haven of peace for various orders of monks. To preserve their absolute peace – so says a local legend – they even ordered the more vociferous of the birds (nightingales, blackbirds, thrushes) to abandon the district. They built a wall to keep out intruders – especially women who, by a papal bull of 1622, were threatened with excommunication if they dared to pass the gate. Its text, and the text of a further bull of 1643 promising similar punishment for anyone damaging the trees, can be seen on the façade of the Coimbra Gate in the perimeter wall. But one woman at least defied the sex-discrimination – the 'poor, plain Catharine', Queen-Consort of Charles II of England. She, of course, had

some influence in Portugal for she was the daughter of the king (João IV, 1640–56). In order that she did not 'pass the gate' of the only entry then existing they cut another gateway (still called the Queen's Gate) specially for her.

Amid the lovely trees are fountains, waterfalls, a lake, a stream, 10 hermitages, a *via sacra* or way of the cross winding along a forest path to the *cruz alta* (from which there is a formidable view), and a former royal hunting lodge, finished by Manuel II 'the Unfortunate' in 1909 only a year before his abdication, now converted into an hotel and surrounded by beautiful gardens. There are also the remnants of a Carmelite monastery, the gloomy monks' cells insulated with local cork against the winter cold. One of the cells was occupied by Wellington the night before the battle of Buçaco (Bussaco in English accounts) and the huge cedar tree nearby was planted personally by the general as a memento for the prior.

A fairly comprehensive exploration of the park is possible by car but a much fuller one on foot by following the signposted paths. Outside the perimeter wall is an obelisk (another fine view from here) and a small military museum, both commemorating the battle on 27 Sept. 1810 between British and Portuguese forces commanded by Wellington and the French under Masséna. The French attacked, surprisingly, straight up the slope – 'the damned long hill' in the words of a British staff officer – while allied troops waited just behind the ridge. In a few hours, on this lovely, peaceful site – less wooded then – 5700 men were wounded or died. *Coimbra 30km/19mi.*

## Caldas da Rainha               M4

*Leiria* (pop. 16,000) The name means the 'queen's thermal baths' and the queen was Leonor, wife of João II. In 1484 she was passing by when she noticed some country people dipping themselves in pools of water, which smelled unpleasantly of sulphur. She stopped to ask why they were doing it and was told that they were curing their rheumatism. She decided to try the cure herself and was so impressed by the rapidity of the relief it brought her that she set about building a hospital there, selling jewellery and other personal possessions to pay for it. By the end of the 19th century the little town had developed into the most stylish watering place in the country.

The spa stands in a spacious park with gardens, lawns, flowering shrubs, and a lagoon. Also in the park is the museum containing works by the local painter José Malhoa (1855–1933) after whom the museum is named, and some outstanding portraits by Columbano (1857–1929). In the town is the factory founded by the controversial potter and caricaturist Rafael Bordalo Pinheiro (1846–1905) the output of which includes crudely-coloured ceramic fruit and vegetables. See also the Church of *Nossa Senhora do Pópulo*, built by Queen Leonor, Its interior walls are completely covered with 17th-century *azulejos.* Local sweetmeats: *cavacas* and *trouxas de ovos* (literally 'bundles of eggs'). *Lisbon 100km/62mi.*

## Coimbra     H7

*Coimbra* (pop. 40,000) Its picturesque white houses are built on a hill above the River Mondego, 42km/26mi from its mouth. Its university, founded 1290 and the only one in Portugal until the advent of the republic in 1911, is one of the oldest in the world. (Oxford 1249, Cambridge 1284). It is a city that has been eulogized by poets and chided by famous travellers for the dirtiness of its streets and lack of good accommodation. (Today it has six hotels and 16 pensions.) Certainly it has the air of an industrial town (it makes pottery, textiles and much else including toothpicks) rather than that of a seat of learning. Nevertheless it has beautified itself with parks and gardens. The 7000 students of the university no longer wear the long black gowns with notches in the hem to commemorate romantic conquests but their briefcases are still decorated with distinctively coloured ribbons which they ceremoniously burn on graduation day. And they still play guitars and sing their traditional songs, the *fados.* They are also still called to classes by the great bell nicknamed *la cabra* (the goat) that booms from the university tower. Three boisterous students once silenced the bell by stealing the clapper, 'to give the chaps a day's holiday'.

For 116 years (1139–1255) Coimbra was Portugal's capital. It was the birthplace of six kings, and of the poet Sá de Miranda (c1485–1558), the composer Carlos Seixas (1704–42) and the sculptor Machado de Castro (c1732–1822). It was one of the three Portuguese centres of the Inquisition. It was also the centre of a school of sculpture, founded around 1520 and later nationally renowned. Some very fine examples of this sculpture, and of earlier work dating to the 14th century, may be seen in the **Machado de Castro Museum**, situated in the picturesque upper part of the town around the imposing Almeida Arch (*Arco de Almeida*). You can divert slightly to the left, if you wish, to see the lovely 16th-century Palace of Sub-Ripas, now a private residence. In the Machado de Castro Museum, in addition to sculpture, are church ornaments and plate, furniture, embroidery, porcelain, and many valuable paintings. The building was formerly the bishop's palace. Before leaving see the subterranean passages containing Visigoth, Roman, and Neolithic exhibits.

*Old Cathedral, Coimbra*

Nearby, on a lower level, is the **old cathedral** (*sé velha*), the most important Romanesque building in Portugal and having the appearance of a fortress. It was erected 1140–75 under the direction of two French architects, 'Robert' and 'Bernard', by order of Afonso I. The retable of the main altar (1488–1508) is of Flemish workmanship, made by Olivier de Gant and Jean d'Ypres. Here St Anthony of Padua was ordained priest.

The lovely **old university** (now largely superseded by an ugly new one) is open to the public and has an attractive entrance courtyard, the great hall with 17th-century painted ceiling and portraits of past kings, the private examination hall and the three lofty, outstandingly beautiful rooms housing the library of 150,000 volumes.

In the lower town is the **Monastery of the Holy Cross** (*Mosteiro de Santa Cruz*), rebuilt 16th century on 12th-century foundations, with its fine Manueline doorway, pulpit carved 1552 by Jean de Rouen and Nicolas Chanterène, unique 16th-century gilded choirstalls carved by François Lorete and depicting the voyages of the great Portuguese explorer Vasco da Gama (1469–1525). See also in Coimbra, all in the lower part of the town: the Old Convent of St Clare (*Santa Clara-a-Velha*), founded 1286 and now sadly ruined by the silting of the river, the **Children's Garden** (*Portugal dos Pequenitos*) with its miniature houses in various styles, the Botanical Gardens (20 hectares/50 acres, the largest in Portugal) and the *Quinta das Lágrimas*, the 'house of tears' where the lovely Inês de Castro (see Alcobaça) was murdered. *Lisbon 199km/123mi, Porto 116/72.*

*Roman mosaic, Conímbriga*

## Conímbriga, Ruins of    I7

*Coimbra* This is the biggest Roman settlement so far excavated in Portugal (13 Hectares/32 acres) and is enclosed by a wall 1.5km/1mi long, hastily constructed and reusing handy material including broken statuary. The settlement dates from the 3rd century AD but after its destruction by the Suevi around 460 it became obliterated and forgotten until 1900. So far discovered are two large villas with mosaic floors, ornamental pools, baths centrally heated by hypocaust, and complete water supply and sewage systems. There are also a forum, a temple, an aqueduct, public baths – and several human skeletons still left *in situ*. *Coimbra 16km/10mi.*

## Fátima    L6

*Santarém* (pop. 6000) On 13 May 1917 three children said they had seen a vision. They said that the sky lit up and the Virgin descended on to a cork oak tree and spoke to them. Accounts of what she actually said differ. But the children understood that she would appear again on the 13th of every month until October. She did so and on each occasion the attendance grew until for the final appearance, when the rain suddenly stopped and the sun began to rotate in the sky like a ball of fire (though no observatory in the world noticed the phenomenon), the audience numbered 70,000. The Virgin gave a secret message to the children. Part of it is still withheld by papal order. Two of the three children died soon afterwards. The

third in due course became a nun. In 1930 the Bishop of Leiria accepted that an authentic miracle had taken place and authorized the cult of Our Lady of Fatima. Today Fatima rivals Lourdes. Sometimes, in a single day, especially on the 13th of the month, there are half a million pilgrims. In 1967 Pope Paul VI was among them, in 1981 Pope John Paul II. The famous original cork oak tree has disappeared. So has the rustic chapel built in 1919 which someone blew up with dynamite. But there is a huge basilica (containing the tombs of the two children who died, both under 12), convents, hospitals, grottoes, hotels, restaurants, and a whole industry of souvenirs and holy water. *Leiria 22km/14mi.*

## Figueira da Foz    I5

*Coimbra* (pop. 15,000) The 3km/2mi expanse of fine sand at Figueira da Foz is described proudly as 'the queen of Portuguese beaches'. It stands at the mouth of the River Mondego and has an important fishing fleet, a picturesque harbour, a casino, a small museum and the Casa do Paço, an 18th-century house decorated with more than 6000 Delft tiles recovered after a shipwreck. Here, in 1808, Wellington landed his first troops on the beach after the valiant students of Coimbra university had seized the 16th-century fort of Santa Catarina that overlooks the town. *Coimbra 48km/30mi.*

## Leiria    K5

*Leiria* (pop. 12,000) occupies the site of a Roman settlement, was liberated from the Moors in 1135 by Afonso Henriques but recaptured 1147 and its Christian garrison massacred. It was Afonso who built the castle which King Dinis (1279–1325) converted into a royal residence, now again partly restored and open to the public. It was also King Dinis, 'the Farmer', who cared for and extended the great pine woods (10,000 hectares/25,000 acres) to the west of the town. *Coimbra 71km/44mi.*

## Marinha Grande    K5

*Leiria* (pop. 5000) In this small industrial town, surrounded by the huge forest planted by King Dinis (1279–1325) as protection against soil erosion, is a glass factory founded in 1748 by an Englishman, John Beare. In 1769 it was taken over by William Stevens, subsidized by Prime Minister Pombal with a loan of 80,000 *cruzados* and permission to cut wood in the forest, and bequeathed to the Portuguese State when Stevens' brother died in 1826. In the factory is a small museum containing specimens of the company's work. *Leiria 12km/7mi.*

# Nazaré       **L4**

*Leiria* (pop. 9000) Here is a town which
people visit not to see its monuments but
its inhabitants – the fishermen and their
wives. It is said – and their grey eyes and
straight noses seem to confirm it – that
they are of Phoenician descent. The men
wear gaily-coloured tartan shirts and
trousers (often patched) and black caps
like long stockings. The women wear
black kerchiefs on their heads and seven
pleated skirts if single or two if married,
one over the other. Widows wear un-
relieved black and, in winter, a long black
cape. Barefooted, in two files, men and
women carry the laden nets between them
up the beach. As there is no harbour, the
boats also have to be hauled up the beach
each afternoon – by tractor now and not,
as in the past, by oxen. The kaleidoscopic
boats, rounded and curved up, have eyes
painted on the prows.

A road and a funicular railway lead to
the cliff-top quarter of **Sítio** (height
110m/360ft) where a 17th-century chapel
occupies the site of a hermitage erected in
1182 by Fuas Roupinyo in gratitude to the
Virgin for saving him from following a
deer over the cliff while he was hunting on
horseback. *Lisbon 120km/74mi.*

*Fishermen of Nazaré, top: beach at Nazaré, btm*

*Óbidos and its town walls*

## Óbidos                                 N4

*Leiria* (pop. 5000) This is one of the
loveliest little towns in Portugal, and one
of the most visited. It is still surrounded
by the well-cared-for wall, with round
towers and bastions, built by the Moors
but repaired and strengthened many times
since Afonso Henriques drove them out in
1148. The picturesque white houses clus-
ter close together and overlap but still find
space for terraces and gardens. They are
as enchanting today as they or their predecessors were in 1282 when the eight-
year-old Isabel of Aragón received the
town as a wedding present from her 21-
year-old husband, King Dinis. (For 550
years, until 1832, every Portuguese queen
inherited the town.) It was Dinis who
built the castle which later became a royal
residence and is now a *pousada*. In the
town's lovely main square, the 17th-
century **Church of St Mary** (*Igreja de
Santa Maria*), whose interior walls are
tiled, contains a painting of the *Mystic
Marriage of St Catherine* by 'Josefa de
Óbidos' (1634–84), the talented artist-
etcher-modeller-silverworker-caligraph-
er who was born in Sevilla but lived all
her life in Obidos. In this church in 1441
another child bride, also called Isabel, was
married. She too was eight and her husband, Afonso V, who was her cousin, nine.
He had inherited the throne at six. In the
museum, under the patronage of the Gulbenkian Foundation, is a collection of arms
used in the Napoleonic War. *Lisbon 9 4km/
56mi.*

*Inside Óbidos*

*Harbour, Peniche*

## Peniche        N3

*Leiria* (pop. 14,000) The country's fourth biggest fishing port stands on a massively rocky site surrounded by sea except for a sandy isthmus (affording good bathing). It has a canning factory and a dockyard and is noted for lobsters and lace. Here in 1589 the British admirals Drake and Norreys put ashore 1200 men to inflict damage on the Spaniards who were then in occupation. The 16th–17th-century fortress or citadel is surrounded by a well-preserved wall with four gates. During the 36-year dictatorship of Oliveira Salazar (1932–68) it was used as a political prison. *Lisbon 96km/6omi.*

## Pombal        J6

*Leiria* (pop. 12,500) This is a market town which still has the ruins of a castle built by Gualdim Pais, Grand Master of the Knights Templar, about 1175. But it is better known because Portugal's most famous prime minister took its name for his title when made a marquis in 1770. Here seven years later, dismissed and disgraced, he returned to his house in the main square, where he died 8 May 1782. *Coimbra 43km/27mi.*

## Torres Vedras        O3

*Lisboa* (pop. 15,000) This is a nice enough little wine-making town that found itself in the history books because Wellington decided in September 1809 to start build-

ing his 'secret lines' here for the eventual defence of Lisbon (though when the French discovered them about a year later they prudently refused to oblige him by attacking). The defences consisted of 152 hill-top forts and earthworks in two widely-separated lines stretching 40km/25mi to the coast. Some of them can, with difficulty, be traced today. Two miles to the southwest, at **Zambujal**, is one of the most complex prehistoric sites in all of Iberia. *Lisbon 53km/33mi.*

## Vila Nova de Ourém        L7

*Santarém* (pop. 5000) The 'new town' – is an undistinguished agricultural centre completely eclipsed by the 'old town', **Ourém Velha**, 4km/2.5mi southwest. Crowning the hill on which the fortified old town stands is a very much altered and enlarged 13th-century castle, from which you can see the sanctuary of Fatima. Here in 1246 Queen Mécia López de Haro, Spanish wife of Sancho II, was held captive (not too unwillingly, it is said) by a group of noblemen led by the Bishop of Braga's brother. Here also in the 15th century an illegitimate son of João I, Count Afonso of Ourém, built a palace of great luxury. His coat of arms is on the fountain at the entrance to the town and his ornate white marble tomb (1485) can be seen in the crypt of the parish church, rebuilt 1756 after the Lisbon earthquake. *Leiria 25km/16mi.*

# LISBON & ITS COASTS

The great River Tejo or Tagus, on which Lisbon so majestically stands, flows only about a third of its 800km/500mi length inside Portugal. The rest winds through Spain, where it has its source. It divides the Lisbon region in two. North of it are the historic towns of Sintra, Mafra, and Queluz where a succession of monarchs built their summer palaces, all within easy reach of the capital and with no river to cross. On the other hand, the major town of Setúbal had been accessible from Lisbon only after crossing the wide Tejo estuary by boat or by making an enormous détour of 118km/73mi to cover an effective distance of 54/33. But since 1966 the modern suspension bridge and motorway

*Portinho; inset Lisbon from Edward VII Park*

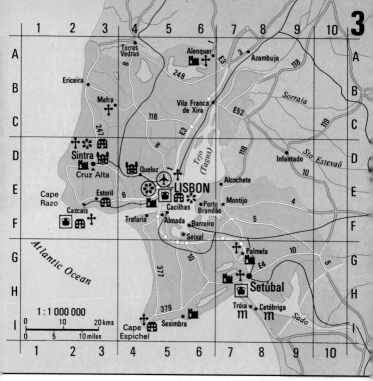

have changed all that and you can now reach the lovely Setúbal coast, or the breathtaking corniche road of the Serra da Arrábida, in little more than half an hour. This is where the delicious Arrábida milk cheeses come from and the famous Azeitão wines that are shipped to the USA in large quantities. Wines produced in this Lisbon region were sent abroad long before those of Porto. Indeed they were mentioned by Chaucer (whose father was a vintner). It is said that the vines of Colares, because their roots go 3m/10ft down into the sand, were the only ones in Europe to resist the *phylloxera* plague accidentally introduced from the USA about 1860. The other well-known vineyards – those of Carcavelos for example – are gradually diminishing in size as tempting prices for land are offered by tourist developers. This lovely coast west of Lisbon – now known as the Estoril coast – was practically unknown to foreigners when the Second World War ended. A good way of seeing it (outside of the commuting hours of 0800–0900 and 1700–1900) is by train, for the line runs from Lisbon all the way beside the sea.

**Fairs and festivals** All year, 1st Sunday each month: Azeitão (Setúbal) – livestock and general fair. 2nd and 4th Sunday each month: São Pedro (southeast outskirts Sintra) – open air market. June (12–13 St Anthony, 23–24 St John, 28–29 St Peter): Lisbon – festival of Popular Saints; dancing, grilled sardines and cold rice pudding. July (1st week) to 1st week Aug.: Estoril – handicrafts fair, cuisine, folk dancing. July 5–6: Vila Franca de Xira – festival of the *colete encarnado* (red waistcoat) traditional dress of the *campinhos* or bull herdsmen, who dance the *fandango*. Running of bulls through streets; popular amusements. Aug. (2nd Sat. for three days): Alcochete – festival of the *barrete verde* (green cap) dedicated to salt pan workers and bull herdsmen; bullfights and running of bulls through streets, blessing of fishing boats, folk music. Sept. (1st week): Palmela – grape festival, bullfights and running of bulls through streets; setting the castle on fire (with fireworks). Sept. 15–20: Setúbal – festival in memory of the famous Portuguese poet Barbosa du Bocage (1765–1805); folk dancing and singing, sports, bullfights.

## Alenquer                     A6

*Lisboa* (pop. 10,000) This is an industrial town but a most attractive one, built on the side of a hill with the river below. The Church of São Francisco is part of the oldest Franciscan convent in Portugal. It was founded c1220 by Sancha, daughter of Sancho I and his queen, Dulce ('Sweet') of Barcelona, and still has one of the original doorways. Nearby are the ruins of a 13th-century castle. *Lisboa 47km/29mi.*

## Cascais                      F2

*Lisboa* (pop. 20,000) Since King Luis and his queen chose this lovely fishing port, with its sandy beaches and gentle climate, as their summer residence in 1870, Cascais has never looked back. It has grown today into an important resort, with a most attractive pedestrians-only shopping centre. Since the monarchy ended in 1910 the royal palace within the old fortress has become a residence of the president of the republic. The rather ugly Palace of the Counts of Castro-Guimarães, now a library, is worth visiting for its antique furniture and porcelain, as is the Church of the Assumption (*Nossa Senhora da Assunção*) for its paintings by the versatile Josefa de Óbidos. There is an open-air market every Wednesday. 10km/6mi west is the **Boca do Inferno** (Mouth of Hell), a rock formation which magnifies the sound of the waves, and, just beyond it, the long sandy, often-deserted, beach of Guincho, The tide can be dangerous at both places. *Lisboa 25km/19mi.*

*Cascais*

## Ericeira B2

*Lisboa* (pop. 3000) This is a village of colour-washed houses mostly on top of a cliff that is strongly buttressed against the Atlantic waves, with a fishing port and a whole series of sandy beaches below. Local restaurants are famed for serving appetizing dishes based on lobster from nurseries among the rocks. It was from here on 5 October 1910 that Manuel II, last of Portugal's kings, sailed away to exile in England and to devote himself to collecting books. *Mafra 10km/16mi. Sintra 22km/14mi.*

*Ereceira*

## Estoril F3

*Lisboa* (pop. 17,500) Estoril has been called the chosen land of exiled monarchs and it is, without doubt, the most elegant of Portugal's many lovely resorts. It has sunny beaches, benevolent winters, luxurious villas, golf, riding, regattas, palm trees and gardens, horse and car racing, and roulette and baccarat at the largest casino in Europe (there are 200 croupiers).

*Estoril, the casino*

*Praça dom Pedro IV, the 'Rossio'*

*April 25th Bridge*

## Lisboa                                    E5

*Lisboa* (pop. 850,000) This is one of the world's most beautiful capitals. It is a city of sun and flowers, of palms and bougain-villaea signifying frost-free winters, of peacocks in the public parks, and of friendly people. It is built attractively on seven low hills, along the wide estuary of the River Tejo or Tagus, 10km/6mi from the sea. It has one of the busiest ports in Europe, big enough for tankers and ocean liners. The great suspension bridge, originally called the Salazar bridge but rapidly changed to **Ponte 25 de Abril** after the 1974 coup d'état, is the longest in Europe (2278m/7474ft, nearly 1.5mi) but 870ft shorter than the Mackinac Straits Bridge at Michigan, USA. Its 79m/259ft foundations, right down to solid rock, are the deepest in the world. From it, or from the ferry boats that cross the river at several places, you get an entrancing introductory view of the lower, newer Lisbon and of the old, higgledy-piggledy town above it.

They say that Ulysses discovered this heavenly site on his long journeyings

*Tram, near the Cathedral*

*Flowerseller in the 'Rossio'*

*Old city and the Castle of St George*

while his faithful Penelope wove her never-ending web at home. Another legend says specifically that Abraham's grandson Elishah founded the city in 3259 BC. More credible is that it was first settled by the intrepid, peace-loving Phoenicians after they had braved the unknown Atlantic beyond the twin Pillars of Hercules (Gibraltar and Ceuta) about 1000 BC. They made their homes on what is today called the Hill of São Jorge (St George), as did the Romans 800 years later, and the Visigoths about AD 415.

When the Moors arrived in 714 they strengthened the castle the Visigoths had built and stayed until 1147. They were ejected, after a four-month siege, by Afonso Henriques, with the help of a large contingent of Anglo–French–German crusaders sheltering here from a gale on their way to the Holy Land. Lisbon became the country's capital in 1255, when Afonso III moved from Coimbra. In the 14th century its great protective walls had 77 towers and 38 gates. In the 16th century, as its ships returned to port

*Elevador Santa Justa*

laden with gold, silk, spices – and slaves – from the new colonies, Lisbon became one of the most prosperous cities in the world. Its population doubled in 30 years. But in the 18th – in 1755 – a tremendous earthquake destroyed two-thirds of the city. It wrecked the work of 1000 years in six seconds. The date was 1 November, All Saints' Day, and the packed congregations were crushed by falling roofs and steeples. Fires started and were propagated by high wind. The terrified survivors fled to the river for safety. But here a tidal wave 12m/40ft high engulfed them and capsized the ships in port. The royal family camped out in the grounds of their shattered palace. The man of the moment was Sebastião de Carvalho e Melo, Marquês de Pombal, later to become prime minister. 'We must bury the dead and feed the living', he said. He also cleared away the rubble and laid out the **Baixa**, the lower town, in the straight lines and rectangles, that you see today. Like all great cities, Lisbon is spreading and names its thoroughfares after friends. There is an Avenida dos Estados Unidos da América and a Rua Washington, a

Praça de Londres and an immaculately-kept landscaped park named after Edward VII of Britain (**Parque Eduardo VII**) (No. 3 on street plan), with its curious **Estufa Fria** or 'cool greenhouse'.

Lisbon was the birthplace of many eminent and famous men. Among them: St Anthony de Padua (1195–1231), the great missionary who, it is said, preached to the fishes when men refused to hear him; Luís de. Camoens (1524–80), Portugal's greatest poet, who lost an eye while serving in Ceuta, was imprisoned for disorderly behaviour in Goa and again here in Lisbon, and died in poverty; Francisco de Almeida (1450–1510), Viceroy of the Indies, who 'died in an affray with savages' where Cape Town stands today, and João de Castro (1500–48) also Viceroy of the Indies; the poets António Ferreira (1528–69) and Alexandre Herculano (1810–77); and the Marquês Pombal himself (1699–1782), virtual dictator of Portugal for 26 years, who kept his nerve in the earthquake when others, including the king, lost theirs, who checked the Inquisition, banished the Jesuits, abolished slavery in Portugal's colony, Brazil, brought riots in Porto to a speedy end by handing out 26 death sentences, accused the noble Távora family of attacking the king, had them broken on the wheel, then burnt to death, revitalized the country's economy – and quickly lost his job when the pious Maria came to the throne.

There are many pleasant ways of exploring this enchanting city – by yellow tram, green-roofed taxi, funicular railway, double-decker bus, metro and even an elevator, **Elevador de Santa Justa** (8) designed by the famous Eiffel. You can wander independently or join a half-day or whole-day guided tour. (Tickets from hotel porters or travel agents).

Lisbon is full of tremendous vistas which can be enjoyed from many parts of the city and from specially constructed vantage points (*miradouros*). The lovely main square, where the government offices are, is the **Praça do Comércio** or **Terreira do Paço** (15) bordered on three sides by majestic arcades and on the fourth by the river. In the centre is the huge equestrian statue of José I, designed by the famous sculptor Machado de Castro. The biggest statue in the world at that time (1774), it contains 38,182kg/37.5 tons of bronze which a certain Brigadier da Costa cast in eight minutes. (No one knows what the hurry was.) Another piece of useless information: the massive marble base was hauled from the quarry by 80 pairs of oxen. The statue long ago prompted Anglo-Saxon residents to nickname

*José I statue in Praça do Comerco, and Arco do Triunfo*

the *praça* Black Horse Square. Through the **Arco do Triunfo** (14) that leads off the praça and at the end of the Rua Augusta, one of Lisbon's best shopping streets, is the **Praça Dom Pedro IV** or **Rossio** (9), a busy, cosmopolitan square with cafés, fountains, and flower stalls. Here, years ago, bullfights were held and, under the Inquisition, heretics were burnt at the stake. The statue, so the story goes, is not of Dom Pedro at all but of the Mexican president Maximilian (1832–67) who was shot before the statue arrived, and Lisbon's municipal council bought it up cheap and renamed it. Nearby is the **Praça dos Restauradores** (6) commemorating the restoration of Portugal's independence in 1640 after 60 years of Spanish rule. From it starts the grand **Avenida da Liberdade** (4), one of the most impressive of all Lisbon's thoroughfares, 1500m/1mi long with 12 lanes of traffic.

In contrast to the modern town-planning of the *Baixa*, the colourful old quarters of **Alfama** (12) and **Bairro Alto** (7) are a labyrinth of alleyways wide enough for a mule below and shaking

*In the Alfama*

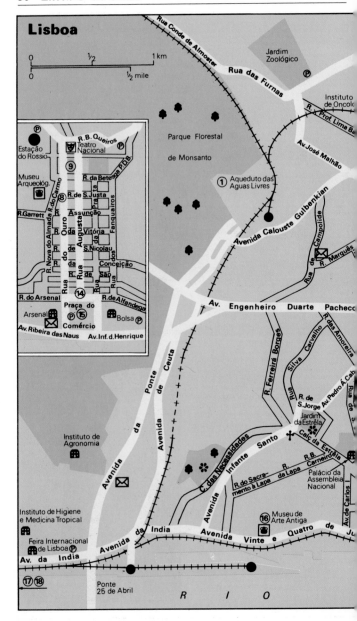

# Lisboa

0       ½       1 km

0        ½ mile

Rua Conde de Almoster

Jardim Zoológico

Rua das Furnas

Instituto de Oncolc

R. Prof Lima Be

Av. José Malhão

Parque Florestal de Monsanto

① Aqueduto das Águas Livres

Avenida Calouste Gulbenkian

R. de Campolide

R. Marquês

Estação do Rossio

R.B.Queiros

Teatro Nacional

⑨

R. da Betesga

P.D.B

Museu Arqueológ.

⑧

R. de S.Justa

R.Garrett

R.Nova do Almada

R.do Carmo

Assunção

Ouro

da

Vitória

S.Nicolau

Rua

do

Rua

de

São

Conceição

Rua

de

Fanqueiros

⑭

R. do Arsenal

R. de Alfandega

Arsenal

Praça do

P ⑮

Comércio

Bolsa P

Av. Ribeira das Naus

Av. Inf. d. Henrique

Av. Engenheiro Duarte Pacheco

Ponte

de

Ceuta

Avenida

da

R. Ferreira Borges

Rua Silva Carvalho

R. das Amoreira

Rua

R. de

S.Jorge

Av. Pedro Á. Cab

Rua de

Jardim da Estrêla

Calç. da Estrêla

Instituto de Agronomia

C. das Necessidades

Avenida

Infante Santo

R. do Sacramento à Lapa

R. da Lapa

R.B. Carneirôla

Palácio da Assembleia Nacional

Instituto de Higiene e Medicina Tropical

Museu de Arte Antiga ⑯

Av. de Carlos

Feira Internacional de Lisboa P

Avenida

da

India

Av. da India

Avenida

Vinte

e

Quatro

de

Ju

⑰⑱

Ponte 25 de Abril

R     I     O

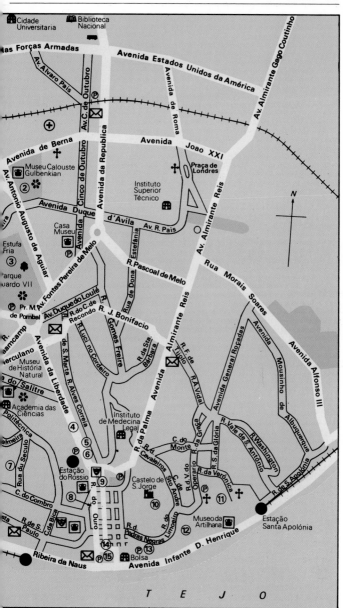

*Tower of Belém*

hands from window to window above. They are fascinating districts of steps, dead ends, street markets, intriguing shops, birds in cages, flowers in pots, Virgins in niches, and washing hanging on lines. Here you will find the 'typical' restaurants and will often be serenaded with guitars and the melancholy songs called *fados*. (There are guided tours of Lisbon by night.)

Despite the 1755 disaster, Lisbon is still rich in architecture and richer still in art treasures. A complete list of museums (some of them dealing with specialized interests such as costumes, folk art, seafaring, music) and of monuments, libraries, gardens, vantage points, hotels, restaurants and public transport can be obtained from the municipal tourist office at Rua das Portas de Santo Antão 141 (5) near the Praça dos Restauradores, or from branch offices throughout the city. But the main places to see are:

**Hieronymite Monastery** (*Mosteiro dos Jerónimos*) (17) in the suburb of Belém (meaning Bethlehem). Founded by Manuel I in thanksgiving for Vasco da Gama's successful voyages 1497–8. One of the finest examples of Manueline architecture. Note the superb south door, the interior in general and the delicate sculptural elegance of the cloister.

**Tower of Belém** (*Torre de Belém*) (18) is the famous 16th-century fortress combining Moorish and Manueline architecture, designed by Francisco de Arruda. Built to guard the entrance to the port, it was from this spot that the Portuguese navigators set off to explore the unknown world – and returned.

While in Belém you could also see the **Coach Museum** (*Museu dos Coches*) containing antique coaches and carriages, including the one in which Philip II of Spain rode to Portugal to take over the throne. (The only other coach from that period is in the Kremlin.)

**Museum of Ancient Art** (*Museu de Arte Antiga*), (16) a very valuable collection of paintings by Portuguese artists such as Nuno Gonçalves (including his famous *Adoration of St Vincent*), Gregório Lopes, Vasco Fernandes, and other great masters such as Raphael, Holbein, Velázquez, Romney, Reynolds, and very many more.

**Cathedral** (*Sé*) (13) Built 12th century, damaged in earthquake, contains several sculptures by Machado de Castro. Until recently the sacristan cared for the supposed descendant of one of St Vincent's two guardian ravens. (See Cape St Vincent.)

**St George's Castle** (*Castelo do São Jorge*) (10) The castle is older than the city itself and has helped to shape its history.

*Monument to the Navigators*

From it you get the best of all Lisbon's views. You can stroll through its attractive gardens, walk on its ramparts, and inspect the great door in which the local hero Martim Moniz wedged his body to prevent the Moors barring it and thus enabled the Christians to enter. From 1300–1500 the castle was a royal residence and several kings were born here.

**Gulbenkian Museum** (2) Calouste Gulbenkian (1869–1955), Turkish-Armenian-naturalized-Briton, whose minority interest in many of the world's petroleum companies earned him the nickname 'Mister Five Per Cent', left his fabulous collection of art treasures to Portugal, where he spent the last 13 years of his life. Here they are.

If in your travels you catch a glimpse of what George Borrow called 'the waterworks', whose 'gigantic arches stalk over the valley like legs of Titans', you may like to know that this great **aqueduct** (1), built 1729–48, 18.5km/12mi long, still brings water to the city.

Finally, the **flea market** (*feira da ladra*) is held on the Campo de Santa Clara (11) on Tuesdays and Saturdays.

*Flea market in Campo de Santa Clara*

## Mafra B3

*Lisboa* (pop. 4000) In 1276 a former parish priest of this little town was elected pope – John XX. But he insisted upon being known as John XXI because, he said, one of his predecessors had not been counted. He meant the legendary female pope, Joan (c855–8), thought to have been of English parentage, who passed herself off as a man, becoming John VIII. But Mafra's far greater claim to fame lies in the colossal, rectangular monastery which Joao V intended should outshine Philip II's Escorial, near Madrid. João built it in fulfilment of the vow he had made in exchange for divine assistance in the production of an heir to the throne. After three years of marriage to Marie-Ana, sister of Archduke Charles of Austria, there was no sign of offspring. But within a year of his vow, in 1711, a child was born, but a girl, Maria Barbara. (Instead of becoming Queen of Portugal she became Queen of Spain, by marrying Fernando VI, who worshipped her.) But three years later came a boy, José, who in due course (after a 34-year wait) was to succeed his father as king. João was more than satisfied and in 1717 started building. He engaged a German architect, Johann Friederich Ludwig, who had already been brought to Portugal by the Jesuits. The ground plan covered four hectares/10 acres. The work took 18 years and at one time 45,000 craftsmen were employed on it. A special hospital was built to deal with accidents and illness. Materials and adornments were brought from the Netherlands, Belgium, France, Italy, in addition to millions of tons of stone from nearer home. Expense was no object, for gold and other treasure was flowing in from Portugal's colony, Brazil. Someone has counted the windows and doors and testifies that they total 4,500. But Byron described the resulting monument as 'magnificence without elegance'. In the centre of the main façade (220m/722ft) is the huge church with its shallow, semicircular entrance steps and enormous statues. The interior is notable for its elegant proportions, for the use of different coloured marble and for the lovely rose-tinted cupola 70m/230ft high. There are no fewer than six organs. In the church towers is a carillon of 114 bells, the biggest weighing ten tons. They produce a symphony of sound audible miles away.

To visit the monastery itself you must join one of the guided tours. You can then see the museum of sacred art, the pharmacy with its rather forbidding collection of antique surgical instruments, the hospital in the form of a church with 16 beds from which the patients could hear mass, the kitchens (if not still occupied by the military), the royal apartments (in which João VI sought escape from his wife's hatred and Manuel II 'the Unfortunate' spent his last night before going into exile in 1910) and the cells which at one time accommodated 280 friars and 150 novices. You can also see the enormous welllighted library of 30,000 volumes with its students' alcoves – 'except for the university library at Coimbra the most beautiful room in the world'. *Lisboa 40km/25mi.*

*Monastery, Mafra*

*Summer Palace, Queluz*

## Palmela         G8

*Setúbal* (pop. 10,000) From the gigantic castle there are some of the best views in all Portugal – to the green valleys of the Tejo and the Sado, to Setúbal and its windmills, to the beaches of Tróia, the vast open sea and, if the air is clear, the distant white houses of Lisbon. In this castle João II (1481–95), forestalling a plot to overthrow him, summoned the leader of it, the Duke of Viseu, and personally stabbed him to death. The Bishop of Évora, also implicated, was locked in the dungeon where he died within a week. Inside the castle precincts is the Monastery of São Tiago (St James), part of which is now a *pousada*. In Palmela they make the delicious, sweet moscatel wine.

## Queluz         E4

*Lisboa* -pop. 29,000) If the royal residence of Mafra is cold and austere, the Queluz palace has at least some of the elegance of Versailles. It was built 1747–52 by Dom Pedro, second son of João V. It was intended as the main country residence of the royal children. One of them, Francisco, died here from 'lobster indigestion' and his ghost is said to haunt the gardens 'in redemption of his sins'. Dom Pedro

himself, by special dispensation of the pope, married his own niece, the future Queen Maria (1777–1817), who made the Queluz palace her home. Here she lived to the age of 82. In the last 30 years, after Pedro's death, she was demented.

The architect of the palace was Mateus Vicente de Oliveira but the Frenchman Jean-Baptiste Robillon added to it in 1758 and also designed the outstandingly attractive gardens. In hot weather the queen would sit here with her feet in the water of the fountain. When the palace is not occupied by visiting heads of state, a guided tour enables one to see the guard rooms (in one of which is a 16th-century Arraiolos carpet), the hall of mirrors, the luxurious throne room with its crystal chandeliers, the hall of the ambassadors (damaged by fire in 1934 but restored), the music room, the tiled room with its Hepplewhite armchairs, the council room, the dining room, the chapel, the breakfast room containing paintings of royal picnics, the rooms of the three princesses, the queen's dressing room, the king's bedroom decorated with scenes from *Don Quixote* and in which Pedro VI (1798–1831) was born and also died. The palace kitchens are now very appropriately used as a public restaurant. *Lisbon 14km/9mi.*

## Sesimbra                                   I5

*Setúbal* (pop. 17,500) This is nowadays a popular holiday resort but its main activity is still, as always, fishing. Each afternoon its colourful boats with eyes painted on their prows return to unload their catches on the beach, where they are auctioned immediately. Sesimbra is also a main centre for big game fishing – tunny, swordfish and shark. A tunnyfish weighing 246kg/nearly 5cwt has been caught here. And if you wish to try a firm, tasty swordfish steak (*bife de espadarte*) or even a fish stew (*caldeirada*) there is no better place than a Sesimbra restaurant. The beach is narrow but long and is sheltered from the north by the Serra da Arrábida which runs parallel to the coast. *Lisbon 32km/20mi*. To the east (6km/4mi) there is a 1000-year-old Moorish castle (partially restored 1940) from which there is a wide panoramic view over land and sea. West from Sesimbra (12km/7.5mi) is the desolate **Cape Espichel** with its lighthouse and famous shrine of Our Lady of the Cape (*Nossa Senhora do Cabo*) which has been a place of pilgrimage for centuries.

## Setúbal                                    H8

*Setúbal* (pop. 59,000) Legend (or perhaps a joker) attributes the founding of this city to Tubal, grandson of Noah, one of the seven sons of Japhet whom Noah begat when he was a youthful 500 – he lived, you will remember, to 950. It stands on the wide estuary of the River Sado, was a Roman town and a place of some importance by the time Afonso Henriques became Portugal's first king in 1139. It is a lovely city. The Danish storyteller Hans Andersen called it a 'terrestrial paradise' in 1834, a more contemporary writer 'the most romantically beautiful seaside resort in Portugal'. (The Portuguese themselves used to describe the mountain approach road as 'the route of the rocks of gold' but

what they had in mind was the enormous cost of making it.) The town is well known for the sea salt produced by evaporation, for the rice from its paddy fields, for oranges, moscatel grapes, canning factories and for its fishing fleet of 2000 boats (the third in importance in the country), for shipbuilding and, nowadays, motor cars. The river estuary is also a nursery for oysters, most of which are exported to France as 'seed'. Setúbal was the birthplace of the poet Manuel du Bocage (1765–1806), remembered chiefly for his sonnets, and of the singer Louisa Todi (1754–1833).

The Church of Jesus (*Igreja de Jesus*) was founded about 1490 by Justa Rodrigues, mistress of Manuel 'the Fortunate' but work did not start until 1494. It was the first church to embody the 'Manueline' style of architecture (see p. 9) which you see on the twisted stone pillars and spiral ribs of the vault. Its architect was Diogo Boytac, who later worked on the famous Hieronymite monastery of Belém. Adjoining the church and housed in the monastery cloisters is the municipal museum (archaeology, antique furniture, coins) and, in the upper galleries, Portuguese primitives including many outstanding 16th-century paintings and the famous retable by an anonymous artist known simply as the 'Master of Setúbal'. A Manueline doorway can be seen in the Church of São Julião. On the western outskirts of the town is the Castle of São Felipe (now a *pousada*) built by Philip II of Spain to repel attacks expected from Portugal's ally England after his usurpation of the throne in 1580. *Lisbon 39km/14mi*. **Tróia**, across the estuary (regular crossings by ferry boats and hovercraft) is a vast, self-contained holiday resort built on a long, sandy peninsula. The ruins of the Roman city of **Cetóbriga**, destroyed by a tidal wave in the 5th century AD, can be seen at low tide.

*Promenade, Setúbal*

## Sintra D3

*Lisboa* (pop. 16,000) 'This fertile Eden,' Byron called it in *Childe Harold* – a green and fertile garden that one reaches suddenly after crossing the barren, rocky *serra*. Southey, Camoens, and Gil Vicente also sang its praises. And to George Borrow it was 'an enchanted region'. Here for six centuries Portugal's monarchs had their summer residence. The palace is still there in all its glory but now called the *Palácio Nacional*. It is Moorish in origin and one of the oldest buildings in Portugal. João I enlarged it in 1415 and it was here that he planned the expedition to capture Ceuta. Subsequent monarchs enlarged it further still. Afonso V (1438–81) was born and died here and Sebastião (1557–78) was proclaimed king at the age of three and here held his last *Cortes* (Parliament) before going to his presumed death in Morocco at the age of 24. (See *Lagos*, p. 84). The mentally defective Afonso VI (1656–83) spent the last nine years of his life locked up by his son, the future Pedro II, who stole his impotent father's French wife. On the guided tour you will probably be shown the flooring worn by Afonso's constant pacing. You can also see the chapel where he died of a fit while hearing mass, the Chinese room containing a pagoda presented to Princess Carlota Joaquina by the Emperor of China in 1806, the *sala dos brasões* or heraldry room painted in 1515 with the arms of 72 nobles (less one who fell into disgrace), the room of the mermaids with extremely rare black tiles round the door, the enormous room of the swans, the dining room, Dom Sebastião's bedroom and the *sala das pêgas* or magpie room. (João I ordered that a magpie should be painted on the ceiling to represent each lady of the court, all of whom had chattered and giggled when they heard he had been caught by his English queen Philippa kissing one of them. Each magpie holds in its beak João's motto *por bem*, for good.)

Under the Convention of Sintra in 1808 the French, defeated by Wellington at Vimeiro, were repatriated on British ships with all their arms (and plunder), an overgenerous act that left everybody, especially the Portuguese, astounded. The house (now an hotel) in which the treaty was thought to have been signed, though there is now doubt, is still called the Palace of the *Seteais* (Seven Sighs). *Lisbon 28km/17mi.*

*Palacio Nacional, Sintra*

*Castelo da Pena*

High above the town (450m/1476ft) and 2.5km/1.5mi by the steep, winding road which affords spectacular views, is the ruined Moorish castle (*Castelo dos Mouros*), built in the 9th century and captured by Portugal's first king Afonso Henriques in 1147. The bodies of those killed in the battle were unearthed (and reinterred) during restoration work in c1850. A little further on, built magnificently on top of a rocky peak, is the Pena Castle (*Castelo da Pena*), a curious conglomeration of architectural styles, built by Ferdinand of Saxe-Coburg-Gotha, the romantic consort of Maria II and cousin of Queen Victoria's consort Prince Albert, on the site of a monastery (of which the chapel and the cloister remain) founded in 1509 by Manuel I. A conducted tour encompasses salons and bedrooms lead-

ing, a little inconveniently perhaps, one out of another, all substantially as they were when last occupied by the royal family. The surrounding park (200 hectares/500 acres) is also open to the public. Nearby is the *Cruz Alta*, (529m/1736ft) the highest point of the Serra da Sintra. 5km/3mi along the road is the *Convento dos Capuchos* which English-speaking visitors have always called the Cork Convent because its 12 cells, hewn out of the rock, were completely lined with cork to keep out the damp. Nearby are the Montserrate Gardens, laid out by Scottish landscape gardeners mid-19th century and planted with a great variety of shrubs and plants, many of them rare. Before leaving the Sintra district you might like to try *queijadas*, delicious little cakes flavoured with cheese.

# THE MOUNTAINS

They used to call Vila Real and Bragança, the two most northerly districts of this region, *Trás-os-Montes*, 'Beyond the Mountains', they were so cut off from the rest of the country. Modern transport and good roads have changed all that and today *Montanhas* is the most rewarding of all Portugal's regions for those who like to get off the beaten track. But the higher parts are too cold in winter unless you go to Covilhã in the Serra da Estrela for the skiing. In this massive mountain range – it is 60km/37mi long by 30/19 wide – is Portugal's highest peak, *Torre* (1991m/6532ft) and highest mountain road (Covilhã to Seia via Torre), passable only in summer. Down somewhat from the high places there is a land of medieval, often primitive villages, innumerable hill-top castles, orchards, lakes and trout streams. You will see large flocks of sheep and goats tended by shepherds in felt hats and woollen capes carrying crooks with which to drive the wolves away. In the depths of green valleys rivers flow towards the sea. The largest wholly Portuguese river, the Mondego, rises here in the Serra da Estrela, and so does the Zezêre.

**Festivals** April (1st week): Idanha-a-Nova (Castelo Branco) – pilgrimage to local shrine, traditional women's songs and dances with tambourines. May (1st Sunday): Monsanto – Ceremony of throwing flowers from castle ramparts (see p. 64). Aug. (3rd Sunday): Miranda do Douro – energetic stick dance of the *pauliteiros*. Aug. (last week) to mid-Sept.: Viseu – international exhibition of farming, forestry, livestock, wines, handicrafts; folklore, concerts, sports, bullfights, dancing, fireworks. Early Sept.: Lamego – pilgrimages, 'triumphal procession of Our Lady of the Remedies', the 'luminous folklore march', battle of flowers, singing, dancing, fireworks.

## Bragança C8

*Bragança* (pop. 12,000) This is an attractive place surrounded by fertile land and barren mountain. It is 680m/2230ft above sea level. The old part of the town is enclosed by tall ramparts and dominated by the great tower of homage of the castle, constructed 1187. The **Domus Municipalis** or town hall, built over a water storage tank, is a gem of 12th-century architecture and has a circular stone seat for the councillors. Nearby is a pillory (*pelourinho*) with a base in the form of a boar and a stone column to which the offenders were tied hand and foot. Bragança has nine churches, most of them

having painted ceilings, the most interesting being that of St Mary (*Santa Maria do Castelo*), 16th-century, depicting in many colours the assumption of the Virgin Mary. It was in the Church of *São Vicente* (St Vincent) that the future Pedro I (1357–67) secretly married his mistress Inês de Castro (see Alcobaça). The powerful dukes of Bragança, whose seat, however, was not here but at Vila Viçosa (see p. 76), were also monarchs of Portugal for 270 years (1640–1910). Catharine, the homely daughter of one of them (João IV), married England's Charles II, 'the most profligate king in English history', though she nevertheless loved him dearly. The **Abade de Baçal Museum**, in the former episcopal palace, is named after a former parish priest at the turn of the century who compiled an 11-volume history of the district. The museum contains a collection of granite pigs, painting, sculpture, furniture, bronzes, and a collection of pre-republic coins. Porto 251km/156mi. Spanish border (Quintanilha) 8km/5mi.

## Caramulo K1

*Viseu* (pop. 2000) You will be surprised to find in a small place like this, 750m/2460ft up in the mountains, two museums of no small importance: a car museum containing 60 cars including an 1898 Peugeot, a 1902 Darracq, and a 1911 Rolls-Royce, all in working order; and the Abel Lacerda Museum containing pictures by Jordaens, Picasso, Dali, Graham Sutherland, Francis Pourbus, Hyacinthe Rigaud and Vieira da Silva, and 16th-century Brussels tapestries. Apart from this Caramulo is an ideal place for a restful holiday and a good centre for exploring the surrounding mountains. *Viseu 45km/28mi.*

## Castelo Branco O5

*Castelo Branco* (pop. 24,000) A town that is known for its olive oil, cheese, wine, and honey – a lovely mixture. But its finely-embroidered *colchas* or bedspreads are lovelier still. Every young lady makes one for her future home and, on her wedding day, spreads it over the bed to display the presents on. The effect is so beautiful that the happy couple have been known to sleep on the floor so as not to disturb it. The show place of the town is not the 18th-century castle on the hill or the old cathedral (now, since 1881, the Church of *São Miguel*), but the gardens of the old bishop's palace (**Jardim do Antigo Paço Episcopal**), with flower beds, urns, obelisks, topiary, and a remarkable staircase flanked by statues of Portuguese kings. The **Tavares Proença Museum** in the episcopal palace itself should also be visited if only for its impressive collection of Castelo Branco bedspreads. *Coimbra 154km/95mi. Spanish frontier (Segura) 58/36.*

## Chaves                                    D5
*Vila Real* (pop. 12,000) Deep below the bare, windy, inhospitable but spectacularly beautiful mountains is a fertile valley watered by the River Tâmega. Overlooking it, on a promontory, is this little town of Chaves, with thermal springs the Romans discovered and a bridge built in the time of the Spanish-born Roman emperor Trajan (c56–117AD), with 12 of its original 18 arches remaining but its stone parapet has unfortunately been replaced with an iron one. Above the town is the castle, built by King Dinis (1279–1325). Its massive tower, today housing a military museum, became the residence of the first Duke of Bragança, illegitimate son of João I (1385–1433). In the main square, the Praça de Camões, is the 17th-century Church of the Misericórdia with its attractive façade and porch, tiled interior and painted ceiling. *Bragança 100km/62mi. Spanish frontier (Vila Verde da Raia) 10km/6mi.*

## Covilhã                                   M5
*Castelo Branco* (pop. 25,000) This town was built on the southern slope of the mountain range known as the Serra da Estrela. There is little to see apart from the remains of a castle, the Romanesque Chapel of St Martinho and a maze of very steep and very narrow streets. The town is nowadays a centre for winter sports and noted for its *queijo da serra* cheese made from ewes' milk. It also has a very important wool industry and supplies more than half the yarn Portugal uses. (In the 17th century carders and spinners came from Essex to introduce English methods.) *Castelo Branco 63km/39mi.*

## Guarda                                    K6
*Guarda* (pop. 15,000) This is the highest town in Portugal (1100m/3608ft) and stands on the eastern slope of the Serra da Estrela. It is described by the Portuguese as *fria, forte, farta e feia* (cold, strong, well-fed and ugly). Its position has always given it strategic importance – in Moorish times, in the wars with Spain, in the Peninsular War against Napoleon. Of its ancient fortifications the 12th–13th-century **Blacksmiths' Tower** (*Torre dos Ferreiros*) and the Menagem Tower or **Tower of Homage** have survived along with stretches of wall and some gates. The grey granite cathedral, first built 14th century, resembles a fortress with its twin octagonal towers. It combines several architectural styles and was completed about 1550. Among its many gargoyles it is said there used to be a very rude one on the side facing Spain. *Coimbra 166km/103mi.*

## Lamego                                    H3
*Viseu* (pop. 11,500) This is a most attractive town of unspoilt baroque houses and is noted for its smoked ham and sparkling wine. The nearby valley of the River Douro is a green and peaceful expanse of maize and vines. Overlooking the town from one hill is the ruined 12th-century castle. On another hill is the remarkable 18th-century **Sanctuary of Our Lady of Redemption** (*Santuário Nossa Senhora dos Remédios*) reached by an enormous monumental staircase of nine landings and 286 steps. In the lower town the central square has been converted into a public garden. Nearby is the cathedral with a west front dating from 1508–15, two organs, some interesting choir stalls and an attractive cloister. The museum, housed in the former mid-18th-century episcopal palace, has an interesting collection of 16th-century Flemish tapestries and several outstanding paintings by Vasco Fernandes ('Grão Vasco', c1475–1541), who used his village friends as models for Christ and his apostles. *Porto 128km/79mi.*

## Miranda do Douro                          E10
*Bragança* (pop. 2000) In this picturesque little town which, as its name says, 'looks over the River Douro' towards Spain, the people speak their own special dialect, *mirandês*. They also have their own special dance, the *pauliteiro* or stick dance, the men wearing white skirts, embroidered shirts and black hats with red ribbons. There are the remains of a castle badly damaged in 1762 by an explosion which killed 400 people. Here in 1813, with the river 'boiling and seething at the bottom

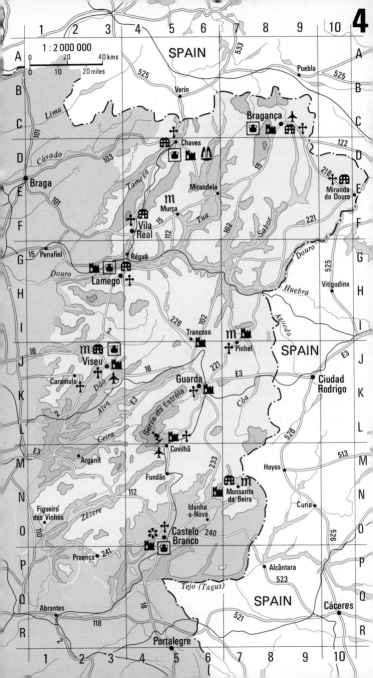

*The Mountains from Serra do Gerês*

*Monsanto villagers commemorate the siege*

*Azulejos decorate a wall in Viseu*

of the ravine', Wellington was winched across in a wicker basket. Today one crosses by the road over the dam. In the old walled town, alongside numerous 16th-century houses, is the austere, granite former cathedral, built 1550–75, and containing an interesting retable (1610–14) by a Spanish craftsman, Juan Murriátegui, carved choir stalls and an amusing little Child Jesus in top hat and white tie. *Bragança 84km/52ml.*

## Monsanto da Beira                N7

*Castelo Branco* (pop. 2500) Although not on the tourist routes, Monsanto has often been described as Portugal's 'most typical village'. Its quaint, often-escutcheoned granite houses blend with their precipi-

tous, rocky-bouldered background, and steep passageways made for nothing wider than a donkey with panniers wind between them. High above the houses and approached by a steep path leading past Celtic tombs cut out of the rock, is the castle, from which there is a panoramic view of the Serra da Estrela and the Carmona dam and reservoir. It was from this castle that the starving garrison used the successful subterfuge of throwing a plump but unfortunate calf over the ramparts to convince the besiegers there was no hope of surrender through starvation. Each year, on the first Sunday of May, the girls of the village commemorate the event by throwing flowers from the castle walls. *Castelo Branco 54km/33mi.*

## Murça F5

*Vila Real* (pop. 1000) The intriguing thing here is a rough stone carving, the *porca de Murça*, the Murça sow. It stands in the public gardens and is possibly Roman, possibly Carthaginian, possibly Iberian. But its significance leaves one guessing, for no one knows. *Vila Real 40km/25mi.*

## Pinhel J7

*Guarda* (pop. 2500) Reached by a winding mountain road, this attractive village near the Spanish border still has relics of its troubled history, including fortified walls with six picturesque gateways and the remains of a castle built by King Dinis in 1312. It also has the churches of St Mary (*Santa Maria*, 14th-century) and *São Luís*, and many fine old escutcheoned houses with wrought iron balconies. In the main square is a pillory. Just outside Pinhel, on the road from Guarda, is a dolmen, the Anta da Pêra do Moço. This is a huge block of granite supported by five stones. *Guarda 29km/18mi.*

*House of Mateus*

## Trancoso I6

*Guarda* (pop. 2500) Built on a hill 900m/2953ft above sea level, this historic little town still has the fortifications that were so necessary in the Middle Ages. Within the double perimeter walls is the castle with massive square keep, rebuilt several times from the 9th century onward. Here on 24 June 1282 King Dinis married the queen-saint Isabel of Aragón, and here in 1388 another royal marriage was negotiated – that of Catharine of Lancaster, daughter of John of Gaunt (who exacted a high price in cash) to the future Enrique III of Castile. In 1810, during the Peninsular War, General Picton (who was to be killed five years later at the Battle of Waterloo) stayed here in the 'Casa Real' and another of Wellington's generals, Beresford, became Count of Trancoso (and Duke of Elvas). *Guarda 48km/30mi.*

## Vila Real F4

*Vila Real* (pop. 15,000) This is a delightful town built on a plateau overlooking the valley of the River Corgo in the Serra do Marão. It has an internationally known motor racing circuit. Here in 1823 the Count of Amarante raised the cry of 'Death to the constitution! Long live the absolute king!' that led to the Miguelite war. It was the birthplace of the navigator Diogo Cão, discoverer of the River Congo in 1482. His house still stands – number 11 in the main street, Avenida Carvalho Araújo. Also in this street are several attractive 17th–18th-century houses and the elegant town hall (**Paços do Conselho**), built originally 1817 as a misericord. The cathedral, a Gothic building later much altered, has an interior of no great interest. Vila Real is noted for its attractive black pottery and for the Mateus rosé wine that is today widely exported. The Mateus manor (3km/2mi south), an ostentatious 18th-century pinnacled residence surrounded by gardens, statues, vineyards and a lake, may be visited. *Porto 116km/72mi.*

*Viseu and the cathedral*

# Viseu                                    J3

*Viseu* (pop. 20,000) One of Portugal's show towns, Viseu stands on the banks of the River Pavia, a tributary of the Mondego. It is an agricultural market town, makes carpets, lace, basketware, and the black *Molelos* pottery typical of the district. But, most of all, it is famous for its Dão wines. It has many fine old houses and the remains of 15th-century walls with the lovely gateways known as the *Arco dos Melos, Arco do Soar,* and *Arco dos Caveleiros.* It was an important place in early Roman times and the tradition is that the humble shepherd Viriatus who raised a private army in defiance of Rome and defeated Plautius, Claudius, and Servillianus (and was poisoned 138 BC by three of his followers bribed by the Romans) built as his last stronghold the circular fortification known as the *Cava do Viriato,* traces of which can be seen on the northern outskirts of the town, together with a statue of him in defiant pose. Another tradition is that Rodrigo (709–711), last of the Visigoth kings, was buried here after his defeat by the invading Moors. It was the birthplace of King Duarte (1433–38), of the historian João de Barros (1496–1570) and probably of one of Portugal's finest painters, Vasco Fernandes (c1475–1541), known as 'o Grão Vasco' (the Great Vasco). Some of his best works (including *St Peter on his Throne* and a *Crucifixion,* formerly in the cathedral) are to be seen in the important Grão Vasco Museum. It is installed in the 16th-century **Três Escalões Palace**, in the upper part of the town, and also contains a series of 14 paintings by members of the Viseu school of painting which flourished in the 16th century. In one of these paintings, the *Adoração dos Magos,* the traditional negro Baltasar is patriotically replaced by an Indian from recently-discovered Brazil. Gaspar Vaz (d.1568), another of Portugal's great painters, is also represented. The rest of the three-storeyed museum is devoted to sculpture (including a very fine 18th-century throne), ceramics, carpets, and antique furniture.

Nearby is the cathedral, a 16th-century enlargement of a 12th-century Romanesque church. Its west front incorporates two towers. Inside, the stone vaulting of the nave is carved in the form of 'Manueline' knotted cables. The 1730 retable, which replaced Grão Vasco's paintings now in the museum, is by Santos Pachego. On the south side of the cathedral is a most harmonious two-storeyed cloister decorated with *azulejos.* The cathedral's very valuable treasures (kept in the chapter house) include a 12th-century gospel, a 13th-century enamelled coffer from Limoges, a 16th-century bronze lectern in the form of a pelican, a sculpture by Machado de Castro (c1732–1822) and embroidered vestments from Macao and Rome. Facing the cathedral across the square is the 18th-century **Misericórdia** whose imposing twin-towered façade promises an interior more interesting than it is. Gastronomic speciality: *papos de anjo* (sugared eggs). *Porto 138km/83mi. Coimbra 82km/51mi.*

# THE PLAINS

These great undulating plains occupy more than a third of Portugal's total area. They are the country's granary and its main producer of olive oil. Here also fighting bulls are bred. You can sometimes see them roaming freely on the ranches beside the River Tejo, docile unless separated from the herd or otherwise provoked. Dotted about the plains are innumerable neglected windmills and remote little towns and villages of white, low-built houses with big chimneys. In winter men, women and children wear long, thick woollen capes with three thicknesses of material over the shoulders, like the habits of friars. The summers are hot and lacking in shade. Some of the houses have no windows, for more than enough air can enter through the door.

**Festivals** Feb. 1–3, Candlemas: Mourão (Évora) – purification of the Virgin; fun fair, fireworks, bullfight. June (1st week): Santarém – the famous Ribatejo fair (livestock, implements), bullfights, processions, folk festival. Oct. (3rd week): Castro Verde (Beja) – Fair, held since 1636, of country crafts, livestock, implements, fruit; amusements. Nov. 9–12 (approx): Golegã (Santarém) – St Martin's Fair of riding and draught horses; merrymaking and roast chestnuts.

*Windmills in Portalegre*

## Abrantes                                    D5

*Santarém* (pop. 10,000) The town stands on a hill above the River Tejo with a bridge linking it to the southern bank. It successfully fought off a Moorish onslaught in 1179, was captured 1807 by the French general Junot (who was made Duke of Abrantes by a grateful Napoleon) and was occupied by Wellington two years later. The castle, approached via quaint narrow streets, was built by King Dinis (1279–1325). It was damaged by an earthquake in 1533 but still has old walls and the remains of a keep, from which there is a wide and pleasant view of the river and the olive groves. Also on the hilltop is the 15th-century Church of *Santa Maria do Castelo* (St Mary of the Castle), now the **Lopo de Almeida Museum** containing 15th–16th-century carvings and statuary, a notable retable, 16th-century *azulejos* from Sevilla and the tombs of the Almeida family, who were Counts of Abrantes. Other things to see: the Church of *São Vicente* (St Vincent), founded 1148 by Afonso Henriques, first king of Portugal, but reconstructed early 17th century, and the huge Church of *São João Baptista* (St John the Baptist), founded 1300 by Portugal's Spanish queen and

*Campinos and bulls in Ribatejo*

saint, Isabel, wife of King Dinis, but much restored 1589. In this church João I heard mass prior to the battle of Aljubarrota in 1385. (See Batalha.) You may care to try the local sweetmeat *palha de Abrantes* ('Abrantes straw'). *Lisbon 152km/94mi.*

The romantic-looking castle of **Almourol**, 18km/11mi west, is built on an island in the Tejo and has a central square tower surrounded by walls and nine round towers. It once belonged to the Knights Templar who received it from Afonso Henriques in 1171 in return for their help against the Moors. The castle has inspired a number of Portuguese romances including *Palmerin of England*, translated by Robert Southey. A boat can be hired to circle the island.

## Arraiolos                          I6

*Évora* (pop. 4000) Built on a hilltop in the vast plain of Alentejo, this little town is famous for its brightly-coloured woollen carpets, though the industry has declined since its heyday in the 17th and 18th centuries, and for its *paios* or sausages. There is a ruined 14th-century castle. *Évora 20km/12mi.* The house where Juliana de Sousa Coutinho, the unwilling bride, was born is 3km/2mi south-east. She became known, as the house is today, as *Sempre Noiva* (literally 'always the fiancée'). See *Évora*, p. 72.

## Beja                               M6

*Beja* (pop. 20,000) Here is a town that was founded by Julius Caesar (100–44 BC), was for 240 years under Roman rule (it was one of the three main Roman centres in Lusitania) and a further 448 years (714–1162) under the Moors. It is a very lovely town of whitewashed houses and clean, cobbled streets. Its well-maintained walls, rebuilt first by the Moors and later by Afonso III in 1252, are mostly on Roman foundations and the arch known as the *Porta de Évora* is of Roman construction. The castle is overshadowed by the massive tower of homage 40m/131ft high built by King Dinis (1279–1325) and having a gallery on three sides just below the summit to afford uninterrupted surveillance of the plain of Lower Alentejo and of the Spanish mountains. The tower's three floors, each with a vaulted chamber, are reached via a spiral staircase. In the castle courtyard is a small military museum. Nearby, from the period between the Roman and the Moorish occupations, there is the unique 6th-century disused Visigoth chapel of Santo Amaro.

The former Convent of the Conception (*Convento da Conceição*), a not-very-

pretty building dating from 1467, is, they say, the place where the famous *Love letters of a Portuguese Nun* were written. The nun was Mariana Alcoforado (1640–1723) and the recipient of the letters the Marquis of Chamilly, a dashing colonel in the French army that was helping Portugal to repel an invasion by Spain. She became his lover but he deserted her. And the letters – passionate, sentimental, reproachful, pleading and finally despairing, all written with moving sincerity – were published in France in 1669 and afterwards translated into almost every European language. They are said to have inspired the 'Sonnets from the Portuguese' by Elizabeth Barrett Browning. Today the convent is a museum and among various paintings (three by Ribera), 16th-century *azulejos*, archaeological objects and 19th-century dresses, there is a window grille through which, it is claimed, the lovesick Mariana talked with her handsome but inconstant lover. The originals of the letters are not in the museum. They have never been discovered. *Lisbon 189km/117mi.*

## Castelo de Vide                    D8

*Portalegre* (pop. 5000) This is an old and attractive spa town of white houses, curious chimneys, flowers, elaborate fountains and tortuous streets leading up to the old quarter on the hill. The higher you climb the older are the houses. Above, in the Jewish quarter, the *Judiaria*, they have remained unspoilt since the 15th and 16th centuries; below, with artistic iron grilles over their windows, from the 18th. (You can admire the beauty of the town from the hilltop Chapel of *Nossa Senhora da Penha* (700m/229ft) on the other side of the valley). Bordering the central square, on the Praça de Dom Pedro V, are the town hall (built 1721), several fine 17th-century mansions, the Church of Santa Maria and the 17th-century Torre Palace, now a hospital, in which the liberal statesman Mousinha da Silveira was born in 1780. In the large castle in 1282 Spanish and Portuguese representatives met to arrange the marriage of King Dinis to Isabel of Aragón, the future saint. The castle was badly damaged in 1704 while being defended by Portuguese and British forces against a Spanish attack and by an explosion the following year. It was repaired in 1710. *Castelo Branco 80km/50mi.*

The old village of **Marvão** (pop. 750) lies 10km/6mi to the east. It is perched on an apparently inaccessible mountain top (865m/2838ft) right on the Spanish border. Because of its strategic position it has been fortified from time immemorial and still has 13th-century perimeter walls,

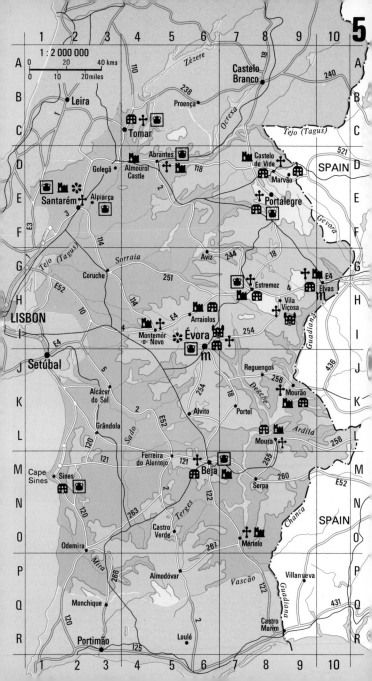

*Roman aqueduct, Elvas*

a square keep and several gates. In this eagle's nest of a town you will see many kestrels.

## Elvas                                    G10

*Portalegre* (pop. 15,000) The first thing you see as you approach Elvas from the west is the enormous Amoreira aqueduct. It was paid for by the townspeople, built on Roman foundations, designed by Francisco de Arruda (architect of Lisbon's Belém tower), has 700 arches, measures 7km/4.5mi in length, was started in 1498, took 50 years to reach the town walls and a further 74 years for water to flow from the lovely Misericórdia fountain which Diogo Marquês designed. Fountain and aqueduct are still in use today. As a frontier town, facing Badajoz in Spain and on the main route Lisbon–Madrid, Elvas has always needed to be more strongly fortified than almost any other Portuguese city. The castle the Moors built is still there today and so is the massive tower of homage built by King João II in 1488. The town's well-preserved 17th-century walls, complete with fortified gates, enclose a roughly rectangular area of 1000m/1094yd by 700m/766yd. Confined tightly within it, in balconied houses lining cobbled streets in some cases no more than 2m/6.5ft wide, lives the not-inconsiderable population. The old cathedral, now, since the bishopric was abolished in 1882, the parish church (*igreja matriz*), has a 13th-century tower but was in the main designed in the Manueline style by Francisco de Arruda and built 1517–37. It has a chancel faced with marble and a massive organ built 1762 by Pasqual Caetano Oldini, an Italian. Elvas has several other churches among them **Freiras de São Domingos**, built 1453–57 in the form of an octagon

*Altar of Freiras de São Domingo*

and later (1659) completely lined with *azulejos*. It stands in the lovely little square (which is in fact a triangle) of Largo Santa Clara, overlooked by iron-grilled windows, a Moorish arch and two 10th-century Moorish towers of the original town wall. In the centre of the square is an interesting 16th-century pillory (*pelourinho*), for all the world resembling an English village cross except that this one still has the irons on which decapitated heads were exhibited. Elvas is well known for olives, garlic sausages, and crystallized plums. *Évora 87km/54mi.*

*Pillory in Largo Santa Clara*

# Estremoz H8

*Évora* (pop. 10,000) This is two towns in one, the lower and the upper. The lower town is newer, though it still has a 17th-century wall with magnificent monumental gateways. In its central square, the Rossio or Praça Marquês de Pombal – 'so extensive that I should think 10,000 soldiers at least might perform their evolutions there with ease', George Borrow wrote in 1835 – stands the town hall, formerly a convent, and the Church of the Misericórdia with a lovely Gothic cloister, and a pillory. Here in the square the colourful Saturday market is held. It is a good opportunity to see and buy the pottery for which the town is famous – jugs, jars, painted figures for Christmas cribs and the typical *moringues* – round earthenware 'bottles' whose porosity keeps water cool by evaporation. Marble too abounds in the district (Philip II of Spain bought huge quantities for his palace-monastery of Escorial) and locally-made marble objects are plentifully available. In the **Museu dos Cristos** is what is claimed to be the world's biggest collection of images of the crucifixion – 1400 of them. The upper town, enclosed by walls Afonso VI rebuilt in the 17th century, is dominated by the great tower, 28m/92ft high, built by King Dinis (1279–1325), inside of which, on the second floor, is a beautiful octagonal chamber. Adjoining is Dom Dinis' palace, now a pousada, where his queen, Isabel of Aragón, died in 1336. (She was canonized by Pope Urban VI 289 years later, in 1625.) In the palace chapel are *azulejos* depicting the famous 'miracle of the roses'. The legend is that the queen-saint, on her way surreptitiously to distribute gold to the poor, is challenged by her suspicious husband but when she opens the folds of her dress the gold has miraculously turned into innocent roses. (It is not on record whether she managed to get the gold back.) *Évora 45km/28mi.*

*Pottery shop*

# Évora
**I6**

*Évora* (pop. 40,000) This very lovely city, built on a hill that rises out of the surrounding plain of Alentejo, is almost completely surrounded by a perfectly preserved 14th-century wall. It has something to show for every period of its 2000 years of history. Here the dissident Roman general Sertorius had a base 80 years BC and you can see today the so-called Sertorius Tower (*Torre de Sertório*). Julius Caesar (100–44 BC) conferred upon the town the title of *Liberalitas Julia* and another Roman emperor, perhaps Hadrian (117–138 AD) or Antoninus Pius (138–161 AD), built the beautiful 'temple of Diana' of granite and Estremoz marble that graces the town today. It is the best-preserved Roman monument of its kind in Portugal – ironically it was preserved by neglect. Generation after generation allowed it to be inundated with rubbish (George Borrow could hardly see it when he passed through in 1835) and it was not uncovered and cleaned up until 1870. Among its majestic Corinthian columns in September 1973 army officers planned the revolution that brought General António Spínola to power seven months later.

The Moors occupied the town for 450 years (715–1165). They were expelled through the strategem of a certain Geraldo sem Pavor (Gerald the Fearless) who staged a diversion on one side of the town while his companions entered from the other. The artistic influence of the Moors on Évora's architecture is evident everywhere and especially in the lovely quarter that still bears their name, the *Mouraria*. For 200 years the town had a university. It was closed down in 1759 by Pombal, Portugal's prime minister and formerly ambassador in London, when he expelled the Jesuits who were running it. But the lovely university buildings are still there, with the attractive 'students' cloister' and classrooms opening from an upper gallery, and are now used as a school. The students still point out the bedroom occupied on a visit by one of the more respectable members of the Borgia family – Francisco (1510–72) who in 1625 was made a saint. Évora became a bishopric in 1540, and one of its early incumbents, Cardinal-Archbishop Henrique, was crowned king in 1578. He founded the university and built the church of São Antão that stands in the main square of the town. In this square King João II watched the execution of his too-ambitious brother-in-law, Fernando Duke of Bragança, and King Sebastião watched victims of the Inquisition burnt alive. The former archbishop's palace is today a museum of sculpture from Roman times onward (ground floor) and of paintings, including work by the Dutchman Ger-

*Temple of Diana and the Cathedral, Évora*

hard David (c1460–1523) and the Spanish-born Portuguese artist Josefa de Óbidos (1634–84), and furniture (first floor). The huge cathedral, with its plain granite façade and unmatched towers, has been described as more interesting than beautiful. It was built approximately 1186–1250, though the chancel was substantially altered c1750. Among the many fine features are the octagonal dome, the rose windows in the transepts, a wooden image of Archangel Gabriel attributed to Olivier de Gant and the massive cloister which was added in 1325. There are several other churches. One, that of São Francisco (1480–1500), has a ghoulish 'chapel of bones' (*capela dos ossos*) whose walls are decorated with 5000 human bones and skulls. It was the idea of a 15th-century Franciscan friar to spur his fellowmen to meditation. Over the entrance are the encouraging words: 'These bones await yours.'

At various times Évora was the residence of Portugal's monarchs. João I (1385–1433) gave his lovely palace, today bearing the name of the Dukes of Cadaval, to his friend Martim Afonso de Melo, who was Évora's mayor. Later it was the residence of João III (1521–57) and João V (1706–50). Part of the palace of King Manuel (1495–1521), who successively married three wives, all Spanish, can be seen in the public gardens.

Another of Évora's historic buildings is the former monastery of *dos Lóios*, built 15th century and now partly used as a *pousada*, and yet another the Convent of the Calvário, built 1570, with an interesting refectory and a two-storeyed cloister. Here the 13-year-old Juliana de Sousa Coutinho, known as *Sempre Noiva* ('always the fiancée'), who happened to be an heiress, was confined for refusing to consummate an enforced marriage to Pombal's son Pedro. After three years her obduracy brought annulment of the marriage and release from the convent to marry her childhood sweetheart Alexandre (who later became Portuguese Minister in London) with whom she had shared lessons from an English tutor, a 'Mr Billingham'.

During the Peninsular War (1808–14) French troops massacred the 'whole insurgent population' of Évora, including women and children. The French commander, General Loison, gave his word of honour to the archbishop that his palace would not be sacked by his troops – and then himself broke cabinets and stole gold and silver medals and the archbishop's ring.

In Évora it is well worth the effort to translate the street names. Such delights as the alley of the Sulking Child and the Square of Our Lord of Earthquakes await you. *Lisbon 145km/90mi.*

*Palace of the Earls of Bastro, Évora*

## Mértola                                    O7

*Beja* (pop. 4000) A lovely small walled
town, with the ruins of a Moorish castle
towering above it. The parish church
(*igreja matriz*), once a mosque, is the only
Portuguese church with five naves. *Beja
53km/33mi.*

## Montemór-o-Novo                          I5

*Évora* (pop. 3000) This was the birthplace
of St John of God (1495–1550), founder of
the Order of Charity, himself so unselfish
that he was thought mad and locked up,
and who, 350 years after his death, was
declared patron saint of all hospitals in
Christendom by Pope Leo XIII. There is
a statue to his memory in the main square
and the parish church occupies the site of
the house in which he was born. The
picturesque older part of the town sur-
rounds the substantial remains of a Moorish castle. *Évora 30km/19mi.*

## Moura                                     L8

*Beja* (pop. 10,000) This town is noted for
olive oil and spa water, many millions of
bottles of which are distributed throughout the country each year. The town's
name is Moorish and the old quarter of
narrow streets and low-built houses with
decorated chimneys in strange shapes still
bears the Moorish name of *Mouraria*. On
the outskirts of the town is the former
Convento do Carmo, the earliest establishment the Carmelites or White Friars had
in Portugal (c1252). An inscription on one
of the tombs in the convent church states
that its occupant died of laughing. Another interesting church is that of St John
the Baptist (*São João Baptista*) which has
a typical Manueline doorway and an unusual series of 17th-century tiles depicting
the cardinal virtues (justice, prudence,
temperance, fortitude). But it is the romantic legend of the castle that interests
most visitors. Although it was rebuilt in
1290 (by King Dinis) and again in 1510
(by Manuel I) and again in 1920, it was the
Moors who originally built it as a defence
against Christian attacks. It was well-nigh
impregnable, so the Christians resorted to
treachery. Hearing that Salúquia, daughter of the local Moorish chief, was to
marry a Moorish nobleman from a neighbouring castle, they ambushed the bride-
groom and his entourage on their way to
the wedding, murdered them and dressed
themselves in the dead men's clothes.
They were thus able to ride into the castle
and capture it. The heartbroken Salúquia
committed suicide by jumping from the
top of the tower. *Beja 48km/30mi.*

## Portalegre                                E8

*Portalegre* (pop. 15,500). With a name like
this – 'happy gateway' – the town ought to
be more interesting than it is. It has a
history going back to Roman times but has
little to show for it. Its 17th- and 18th-
century houses, with their curved
wrought iron balconies and *azulejos*, however, are notable and so is the twin-
towered cathedral with its 18th-century
façade, 17th-century organ and 16th-
century retables. The best of its other old
buildings are put to profane uses (though
entry is permitted). The lovely Convent of
*São Bernardo* also called the Convent of
*Nossa Senhora da Conceição* (Our Lady of
the Conception), founded 1512 by Jorge
de Melo, Bishop of Guarda (whose Estremoz marble tomb, attributed to Nicolas Chanterène, is in the convent
church), is now a police training school.
The Convent of *São Francisco*, which has
a 13th-century church restored in the 17th
century, is occupied by the army. The
Palace of the Counts of Ávila houses the
civil government. The Palace of Fonseca
Accioli is a school, and the convent built
1695 by the Jesuits, whom Pombal in 1759
ejected, is now a tapestry factory. There
is also a museum (sculpture, ceramics,
furniture, paintings, carpets), with iron-
grilled windows, *Palácio Amarelo*, so
called because of its yellow walls, and a
cork factory founded last century by the
American, George Wheelhouse Robinson.
Local delicacy: *toucinho do céu* ('bacon
from heaven'). *Lisbon 238km/148mi.
Évora 103/64.*

## Santarém                                  E2

*Santarém* (pop. 15,000) The town is sup-
posed to have been founded by a certain
Abidis, 'King of the Iberians', about 1100
BC. He called it 'Esca-Abidis' and
Santarém's inhabitants are still known as
*Escalabitanos* today. To account for the
changing of the town's name, it is said that
Santarém is a corruption of Santa Irene.
Irene is a young nun whose dead body
floated 53km/33mi down the river from
Tomar in the year 653 and was washed up
here. One story says that Irene was murdered and thrown into the river by a monk
whose advances she had rejected. Another
says that she did not reject the monk and
was put to death for her sins, then drop-
ped into the river in a marble coffin. But
the coffin miraculously floated, thus prov-
ing her innocence, at any rate to the
satisfaction of the good Christian Visigoth
king Recceswinth (653–72) who, unable to
restore her life (or her chastity), mitigated
the unfortunate error by renaming the
town.

Santarém is the marketing centre for
the prosperous plain bordering the River
Tejo (Ribatejo). It is also a centre of

bullfighting and bull breeding. An excellent view, 'one of the great panoramic landscapes of Europe' according to Palgrave, who came here with Tennyson in 1850, is afforded by the *Portas do Sol* ('gates of the sun') in the walls of the old Moorish castle now enclosing the public gardens. The town once had 13 churches, 14 convents, and 15 hospitals. Quite a number still exist. The Seminary Church (*Igreja do Seminário*) was built by the Jesuits in 1676 and has an unusually large number of niches containing statues of Jesuit saints. The Church of Grace (*Graça*), built 1380–1400, restored 1950, has a very fine rose window, the tomb of Pedro de Maneses, first governor of Ceuta after its capture by João I in 1415, and the tombstone of Pedro Álvares Cabral (c1467–1520), discoverer of Brazil. The bell tower of the Church of *São João de Alporão* was demolished to enable the coach of Queen Maria I (1777–1816) to pass. This church is now an archaeological museum (medieval sculptures, amphoras, *azulejos*, pottery, china, coins) but also contains what some consider to be the best 15th-century tomb in Portugal, that of Duarte Meneses (d.1464), Governor of Ceuta, killed by the Moors, who so mutilated his body that the only thing his distraught wife could retrieve and bring

home was one tooth. That is all the elaborate tomb contains. The Church of São Francisco, founded by King Sancho II (1223–48) and formerly part of a Franciscan convent, now houses a regiment of cavalry complete with horses. *Lisbon 78km/48mi.* In the village of **Alpiarça** (pop. 8000), 10km/6mi east, is the *Casa dos Patudos*, a rather unusual museum containing paintings attributed to Zurbarán, Murillo, Rubens, Van Dyck and what is said to be the only portrait in existence of the composer Scarlatti. There are even British grandfather clocks. All the items were collected by the Portuguese statesman José Relvas (1858–1929) whose house this was.

## Sines                                    M1

*Setúbal* (pop. 8000) This was the birthplace, in 1469, of Portugal's greatest explorer, Vasco da Gama, whose house (almost completely rebuilt) can be seen. Here also, in 1834, after six years of civil war, the usurping King Manuel boarded the British ship *Stag* and sailed away into exile. The local archaeological museum, in a private house, has an interesting display of early jewelry found nearby. There is a minute fishing harbour and several miles of sandy coastline to the south, though the development of the very

*Traditional agriculture in the Plains*

important oil refining and tanker terminal does not add to the beauty of the district. *Setúbal 73km/45mi.*

# Tomar                                    C4

*Santarém* (pop. 17,000) Tomar is a delightful town on a hill beside the River Nabão. It owed its development and prosperity to the Knights Templar who, headed by their grand master, Gualdim Pais, drove out the Moors in 1160 and made it their headquarters until, 147 years later, the Templar order of chivalry was dissolved by Pope Clement V. At the instigation of King Dinis (1279–1325) a new order, the Knights of Christ, was founded to inherit the Templars' wealth and possessions. The great **Convent of Christ** at Tomar perpetuates their name and is one of the wonders of Portugal. It

from the holy sepulchre in Jerusalem. Much of the church's priceless wooden carving (and anything else combustible, including pictures) was piled in the cloisters and burnt by French troops under Masséna in 1810.

See also in Tomar: the Church of St Mary of the Olive Grove (*Santa Maria dos Olivais*) founded by the Templars' grand master, Gualdim Pais (who is buried here but containing little of the original fabric; the Luso-Hebraic Museum housed in the small 14th-century synagogue, the best preserved synagogue in Portugal; and the 180-arched aqueduct built 1593–1614 to bring water to the convent. Tomar is known for its cheeses and *pasteis dos Templários* (Templars' cakes). *Lisbon 143km/89mi.*

*Convent of Christ, Tomar*

*Ancient festival of Tabuleiros, Tomar*

has no fewer than seven cloisters ranging in date from the 12th to the 17th centuries: the main cloister, built 1559–66 by Diogo de Torralva and known also as the *Claustro dos Felipes* because Philip II of Spain is said to have been proclaimed King of Portugal here in 1580; the Ravens Cloister; the small Santa Barbara Cloister; the Micha Cloister where food was distributed to the poor; the Hospedária or 'Lodgings' Cloister; the Burials Cloister and – hygienically but inconveniently on a winter's night, most distant from the lodgings – the Ablutions Cloister. In the centre of the convent is the 12th-century 16-sided Templars' Church whose west front contains Portugal's most famous Manueline window, a sculptural fantasy incorporating ropes, cork floats, anchor chains and seaweed – a reminder that whereas the Templars wielded the sword against the infidel the Knights of Christ explored the unknown world in ships. The name of the craftsman is unknown. The design of the octagonal 'Templars' Rotunda' at the end of the nave is copied

# Vila Viçosa                             H8

*Évora* (pop. 5000) Not, as the name might suggest, a vicious town (*viciosa* would be that) but a luxuriant town, set among dark-green orange trees. It has a great ruined castle dating from the 14th century, built by King Dinis who incorporated parts of the 11th-century castle built by the Moors who in turn had used foundations made by the Romans. But it is to see the grandiose marble-faced **Palace of the Dukes of Bragança** (*Paço Ducal*) that people visit Vila Viçosa today. Its construction was started in 1501 by Jaime, the fourth duke, and finished by his successors. It was the residence of this most famous of all Portugal's noble families for 400 years. Here one holder of the title murdered his wife with a dagger on suspicion of adultery with a servant. Here in 1638 was born Catharine of Bragança who at the age of 24 was to marry Charles II of England at Portsmouth, and here, in 1640, her father succeeded to Portugal's throne as João IV. It was from here in 1908, that Carlos, last but one of Portugal's mon-

archs, set out for Lisbon where he and the heir to the throne, his son, were assassinated. Two years later still, Manuel II left for exile in England, marking the end of the Bragança dynasty of kings. When Manuel died at Twickenham in 1932 he bequeathed his possessions, including the Bragança archives, to his native country. They can be seen in the palace today on a guided tour of the music room, the library, the elegant salons, the chapel, the coach house and the great kitchens which satisfied the gargantuan appetites of guests at banquets, weddings, and bullfights. Near the palace is the gate of the dukes' hunting estate known as the *Tapada*. The wall that encloses it measures *18km/11mi*. See also nearby the Church of *Agostinhos* (Augustines) full of the standardized black and white marble tombs of the Bragança dukes (there is an empty one for Portugal's next king); the Convent of *Chagas* or Poor Clares where the Bragança womenfolk were separately buried; and the *Porta dos Nós*, a curious gateway formed with sculptured knots.

*Manueline Window, Tomar*

# ALGARVE

This popular region of the Algarve (the Moorish name for 'west' – the western part of the Moors' Iberian domain) was completely unknown abroad at the end of World War II. It owes its development to its climate, especially its warm winters, its beauty, and its incomparable beaches. It has 180km/112mi of coastline facing south and another 50/31 round the corner facing out towards the Atlantic. Exotic birds migrate to spend the summer here – hoopoes, bee-eaters, golden orioles – and many more you never see in colder climes There are Mediterranean-type flowers and flowering shrubs everywhere – oleanders, camillias, mesembryanthemum, tamarisk, mimosa, geraniums as big as bushes and rhododendrons growing wild. There are also figs, sugar canes, carobs (which when children we used to know as locust beans), orange trees, pomegranates, and prickly-pear cactus. There is blossom even in winter – in January and February, which in the Algarve is spring. In those months the almond trees bloom. A story the Portuguese tell concerns a Moorish chief who married a beautiful Nordic princess. After a time the princess began to feel homesick because in the Algarve there was never any snow. The Moor bought an almond plantation near Faro, conducted his unhappy wife there after dark one day and when she woke up next morning and saw an expanse of white almond blossom all around and the earth white with petals, she exlaimed in delight that it was more beautiful than any snow could ever be.

Someone once said that the Algarve produces Portugal's best grapes and poorest wine. It is a slander that can be very enjoyably disproved by sampling the wines of Lagoa.

**Festivals** Shrove Tuesday and two preceding days, Carnival: Faro, Portimão, and Loulé – battle of flowers, satirical parade, folk dances. Second Sunday after Easter: Loulé – pilgrimage and return of image of Our Lady of Mercy; singing, dancing, fireworks. July 15–31: Faro – annual fair of everything produced in Algarve; amusements, singing, dancing, fireworks. Oct. 18–23: Faro – annual agricultural, handicrafts and general fair; folk music and dancing groups. Nov. 11–18: Portimão – annual November fair.

*Palm trees, blue skies, white houses – the Algarve*

## Albufeira    G7

(pop. 8000) This was once a stronghold of
the Moors, who here resisted the pressure
of the Christians longer than their col-
leagues in other places, being finally
ousted by Afonso III in 1250. The Moorish character still peeps out occasionally
among the white houses lining its steep
streets. Today the town's main concern is
in developing its tourist industry. It is
already the largest resort on the Algarve
coast. It has a good beach, reached
through the tunnel excavated in 1953
from the main shopping street, and the
less-crowded beaches of São Rafael to the
west and Olhos d'Agua (so-called because
of the fresh-water spring at the very edge
of the sea) to the east. There is a picturesque fishing quarter from which there
are boat trips to neighbouring caves.
*Lisbon 318km/197mi. Faro 35/19.*

## Alvor    F4

(pop. 5000) It is thought that the Carthaginian general Hannibal (247–c182 BC)
founded a settlement here but after that
the town has no recorded history until
1189 when the crusaders, arriving by sea,
slaughtered several thousand occupying
Moors in the sacred cause of Christianity.
King João II (1481–95) made it into a
municipality and came here personally in
1495 on his way to take the waters at the
inland spa of Monchique for his dropsy,
but returned to die. The town is surrounded by tourist developments. Henry

*Fishermen's Beach, Albufeira*

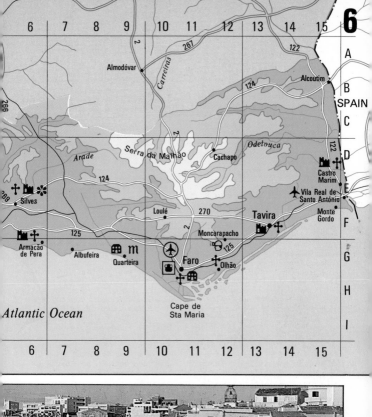

6

A
B
SPAIN
C
D
E
F
G
H
I

Almodóvar

Carreiras

Alcoutim

Serra da Malhão

Cachapo

Arade

Odeleuca

Sílves

Castro Marim

Vila Real de
Santo António

Loulé

Tavira

Monte
Gordo

Armação
de Pera

Albufeira

Quarteira

Moncarapacho

Faro

Olhão

Atlantic Ocean

Cape de
Sta Maria

Cotton designed the 18-hole championship golf course of the Hotel do Golf de Penina and its two 9-hole courses. There is also a casino. *Faro 65km/40mi.*

## Armação de Pêra                    G6

(pop. 2000) This village has an 18th-century fort complete with chapel dedicated to St Anthony, boasts the longest of Algarve's many beaches, and a modern holiday resort has grown up beside it. Early risers may like to watch the interesting fish auction on the beach. There are boat trips to the nearby grottoes. *Faro 46km/29mi.*

## Cabo São Vicente/Cape St Vincent                              G1

This great rocky promontory 75m/246ft high, with the waves pounding it on three sides, is the most southwesterly point of Europe. It is said to have received its name because the body of St Vincent, whose heroism when martyred by order of the Roman general Diocletian in Valencia in AD 403 converted his gaoler to Christianity, was brought here for safety by a party of Christians when the Moors invaded the Iberian Peninsula 300 years later. When 430 years later still Portugal's king Afonso Henriques (1139–85) succeeded in driving the Moors out of this part of the Algarve, the saint's body was taken to Lisbon by sea and legend says that two guardian ravens perched on the ship's rigging all the way, a devotion for

which they found themselves immortalized in Lisbon's coat of arms. After a further 600 years of veneration the saint's remains disappeared in the fire that followed the 1755 earthquake.

The view from the cape is majestic and the lighthouse is the most powerful in Europe (it throws a beam 97km/60mi out to sea). There is also a house, the Vila do Infante, that belonged to Prince Henry the Navigator (see Sagres, p. 86), the Chapel of St Catharine and a cinema showing a film of the great Portuguese discoveries. That is all there is to see. But as you stand there quietly there is much history to recall, so much heroism, so much death. Within sight and sound of these cliffs in 1693 no fewer than 80 English and Dutch ships were sent to the bottom by the French under Admiral Tourville. In 1780 the British admiral Rodney sunk seven Spanish ships out of a squadron of 11. In 1797 Sir John Jervis (later Earl St Vincent after this cape), aided by a young commodore named Horatio Nelson, with 15 sail defeated a Spanish fleet of 27. And in 1832 Sir Charles Napier destroyed a contingent of Dom Miguel's ships during the War of the Two Brothers. But long before this, in 1470, the young sailor Christopher Columbus, serving on a Tunisian galley that was sunk in a battle, was washed ashore here on a plank. He stayed in Portugal 14 years and married an Italian girl in Lisbon. *Faro 128km/70mi.*

*Cape St Vincent*

# Faro H11

(pop. 25,000) Faro is the capital of the Algarve, the centre of its tourist trade, the market for the fruit from the surrounding plantations, and for the sardines, anchovies, tunny fish, and salt from the sea. It has an international airport and a yacht harbour. It is the southernmost point of Portugal and takes its name from the lighthouse (*faro*) originally built by the Moors 1000 years or more ago. It is an old town with almost no old buildings, due chiefly to (1) the Earl of Essex who burnt the whole place down in 1596 to castigate the Spaniards then occupying it, (2) a bad earthquake in 1722 and (3) a worse one in 1755. Essex also helped himself to the bishop's books, which became the nucleus of the Bodleian Library, Oxford. Faro had in fact been a centre of book printing since 1487 when members of the large Jewish community set up a press there. The devastated town was in due course rebuilt under the instigation of its bishop, Francisco Gomes de Avelar (1739–1816). He was responsible for the Arco da Vila, a lovely gateway in the old town, the seminary, the Misericórdia Church, and some of the bridges. He also rebuilt the cathedral, incorporating the only part of it that had survived the disasters, a stubby 13th-century tower. There is a statue to his memory in the cathedral square, and another square, facing the port, is named after him.

The archaeological museum, occupying the restored Church of the Assumption (*Nossa Senhora da Assunção*) contains paintings, porcelain, *azulejos* and Roman objects found locally. There are two other museums – the maritime near the port and the ethnographical (costumes, models, photographs, arts and crafts). The Carmelite Church (*Igreja do Carmo*) has a gruesome chapel whose walls are covered with bones and skulls, its raw material no doubt conveniently emanating from the adjoining graveyard.

There is a ferry service from the harbour to the resort of Praia de Faro built on the long sand bank off the coast. *Lisbon 289km/179mi.*

*Fishermen of Faro*

*Ponta da Piedade, Lagos*

# Lagos      G3

(pop. 1000) An attractive holiday resort at the western end of a wide sandy bay. It is also a fishing port and an international yachting centre. Here Prince Henry the Navigator (1394–1460), son of Philippa of Lancaster and nephew of Henry IV of England, built and refitted the caravels that his captains sailed on their intrepid voyages of discovery. Here too he founded a company to trade with the new empire. The palace that belonged to him is now a hospital and a statue to his memory was erected in 1960 in the Praça do Infante. Another square is named after one of his captains, the famous Gil Eanes who in 1434 rounded Cape Bojador on the coast of Africa. Soon Portuguese ships began to return crammed with African slaves, an immensely profitable business. They were auctioned off under the arcades of the Lagos customs house in the Praça da República. Opposite it is the Church of Santa Maria outside which the bachelor king Sebastião (1557–78) harangued his troops in June 1578 before the disastrous expedition to Morocco where he himself was killed. But was he? There were rumours that he was among the missing (although his supposed remains were brought home) and one opportunist pretender after another came forward to claim the throne – first the son of a potter, then a brigand-insurgent, then a Spanish pastry cook and last an Italian gentleman who in 1603 got himself hanged. Dryden and Zorrilla both wrote plays on the subject.

There are the remains of the old town walls, two forts (one guarding the harbour), an aqueduct built 1490–1521, a small museum (archaeology, ethnography, numismatology, sacred art) housed in the 18th-century Chapel of Santo António in which also is the grave of Hugh Beatty, colonel of an Irish regiment, who died here in 1729. Sheltering Lagos from the west is Ponta da Piedade, a promontory whose orange-red rock has been weathered to resemble a church with arches and spires, with marine caves below. *Faro 8okm/5omi.*

## Loulé F10

(pop. 14,000) This town stands in the hills in a lovely situation 16km/10mi from the sea and is noted for the attractive openwork, Moorish-looking chimneys that crown its white-washed houses. It is also well known for brass and copper work, leatherwork, and embroidery. There are the remains of a Moorish castle. The parish church was presented by King Dinis in 1280 to the Order of São Tiago. *Lisbon 294km/184mi.*

## Monchique D4

(pop. 8000) This lovely little town, nestling 455m/1493ft up in the wooded mountain of Monchique, where baskets, chairs, stools, other wooden objects, and handknitted woollen sweaters are made. Its parish church has a typical Manueline doorway of knotted columns. The peaks of Picota (774m/2539ft) and Fóia (902m/2959ft) afford breathtaking panoramic views. *Faro 83km/51mi. Portimão 22/14.* The exceptionally neat and clean spa of **Caldas de Monchique** whose waters were, as usual, discovered by the Romans, lies 5km/3mi to the south.

## Olhão G12

(pop. 15,000) As you approach you will understand why everyone describes Olhão as a 'cubist' town – the houses are built in white cubes and have two or three storeys with exterior stairs leading to small terraces. The best view of the town is from the tower of the parish church (*igreja matriz*). The town's name derives from *olho*, a spring, from which the inhabitants used to draw their water. It is not an old town. It was founded as recently as about 1700 by fishermen from Aveiro who despaired that anything would ever be done to repair their own port which a violent storm had silted up. (See Aveiro, p. 34.) They set about building their own chapel, *Nossa Senhora dos Aflitos* (Our Lady of Afflictions) with proceeds derived, it has been darkly hinted, less from fish than from the contraband trade with the Spanish port of Cádiz. In the Peninsular War (1808–14) Olhão was one of the first towns to rise against the French. And when they had been driven out of Algarve it was two local fishermen who in their small boat conveyed the glad tidings to the Portuguese royal family who had retired to Brazil. *Faro 9km/6mi.* Near the village of **Moncarapacho**, 9km/6mi northeast are several interesting caves – the huge *Caverna do Abismo* (Cave of the Abyss), *Garrafão*, with thousands of stalactites, and *Coluna* with a colossal stalagmite.

*Harness maker of Loulé*

## Portimão                                F4

(pop. 10,000) This very attractive seaside resort stands at the mouth of the River Arade, has the most important fishing fleet in the Algarve and factories to can the catch of tunny and sardines. The town is also known for its furniture and wickerwork. The Lisbon earthquake of 1755 left it without any old buildings of interest. The resort of **Praia da Rocha**, 3km/2mi west, has one of the loveliest beaches of the whole coast. *Faro 62km/38mi.*

*Sardines at Portimão*

## Quarteira                               G9

(pop. 3000) This is a fishing village that has developed into a major holiday resort, with a long sandy beach bordered by umbrella pines. Nearby is the 1600 hectares/3954 acres tourist centre of **Vilamoura**, the biggest private development in Portugal and one of the biggest in Europe, it is claimed. It has hotels, villages, villas, apartments, riding, tennis, casino, two 18-hole golf courses and a yacht marina for 600 craft, all financed with American, French, and Portuguese capital. Adjoining the resort are the remains of a Roman settlement of some importance. *Faro 20km/12mi.*

## Sagres                                  H1

(pop. 1500) Until the 15th century this was the edge of the known world. In more ancient times men used to watch the sun from here as it fell into the sea and listen for its sizzling cries of agony as it sank. The desolate, rocky, flat-topped promontory is battered by the waves and by winds so strong that almost nothing grows. Here Prince Henry the Navigator (1394–1460) lived for 40 years. Here he

*Fort and promontory of Sagres*

*Praia da Rocha, Portimão*

founded his famous school of seamanship, bringing together the best astronomers and scientists to perfect the astrolabe and sextant, and the best mariners to test them and report to the best map-makers. Here the young Genoese seaman Christopher Columbus added to his skills and might well have discovered the New World for Portugal had not João's rebuff made him go and work for Spain. But the school paved the way for Portuguese mariners to reach India via the Cape of Good Hope. In Sagres today, in the now-restored fort, you can see the prince's school and the house in which he lived (now a youth hostel), the giant compass laid out in stone which helped him with his calculations

and the little chapel of *Nossa Senhora da Graça* (our Lady of Grace) where so often he went to pray and meditate. There is also a plaque presented in 1965 by the US Power Squadrons (a voluntary maritime safety organization) as a tribute to Prince Henry 'whose school of navigation opened the way for world-wide exploration in the great age of discovery'.

## Silves                                   E6
(pop. 11,000) During the Moorish occupation (714–1249) this town, beautifully situated on a slight hill among peach, almond and orange trees, was the capital of Algarve. Though 8km/5mi from the sea it had a port and built ships. At one time it

*Silves; its cathedral and its castle*

had a population of 30,000 and in magnificence and culture outshone Lisbon. But when the Moors were ejected in 1249 (for the second time, for they surrendered through starvation after a three-month siege in 1189 but two years later returned) the place declined. The river port silted up and by the 16th century the population had fallen to 140. Most of the architectural treasures for which the Moors were famous crumbled, or were sacked by Essex (who passed this way in 1596 to punish the usurping Philip II of Spain) or were demolished by the 1755 earthquake. However, much of the town wall, with its gates and towers, and the massive castle, built of reddish-brown local stone, has survived. The castle was restored in 1835 and again in 1940, when its interior was made into gardens. Its huge subterranean cisterns were designed to hold a whole year's supply of water for the garrison. You may like to walk round the parapet. Another massive building that has survived is the cathedral which is 13th-century and occupies the site of a mosque, parts of which can be seen behind the altar. Some of the many tombs the cathedral contains are said to be of crusaders who helped to drive out the Moors. The town also has a Misericórdia church with Manueline side door and to the east is the *Cruz de Portugal*, a 16th-century stone Calvary. *Faro 60km/37mi.*

## Tavira F13

(pop. 10,000) Many people believe this to be the prettiest town in Algarve. It is 23km/14mi from the Spanish frontier and stands near the mouth of the River Gilão. Although its port is now silted up and cut off from the sea by a long spit of land, it is still an important centre of tunny fishing. In April–July large shoals of this giant fish (sometimes 3m/10ft long and weighing 300kg/nearly 6cwt) move down from the Atlantic to spawn in the Mediterranean. This is the time of the *copejo*, the great killing. For now the fish are fat and valuable and those that make the return journey in August will be thin. Barriers of nets are strung across their course and the enmeshed fish, whipping and struggling with tremendous force, are harpooned by the excited, yelling fishermen. The battle can take a long time and the sea become red with blood. But when it is over the tunny is hoisted aboard a fishing boat for its last journey, to the canning factory.

The town of Tavira is divided in two by the river, which is crossed by a seven-arch bridge, originally Roman and repaired in the 17th century. In the older part of the town, narrow streets lead up from the main square, the Praça da República, to the ruined castle from which the view over the rooftops is enchanting. Near the castle is St Mary's Church (*Santa Maria do Castelo*), rebuilt after the 1755 earthquake on a site originally occupied by a mosque. In it is the tomb of Paio Peres Correia who captured the town from the Moors in 1242 and died 1275. There is also an inscription in memory of seven crusading knights of the Order of St James who were out hunting and were killed by the Moors in defiance of a truce, a treachery for which

the already-mentioned Paio Peres Correia exacted angry retribution by assaulting and taking the town. There are several other interesting churches, among them those of the *Misercórdia* and, in the lower town on the other side of the river, *São Paulo* and *Carmo*, both 18th-century. Tavira is known for wine, caramels, and egg-and-almond sweetmeats. There are good beaches at nearby **Santa Luzia** (where a Greek 1st-century inscription was found, unique in Portugal) and the island of **Ilha de Tavira** at the mouth of the river. *Faro 30km/19mi.*

## Vila Real de Santo António E15

(pop. 10,500) This town was founded and built in 1774, in a matter of months, by that dynamic and controversial prime minister Pombal (1699–1782). The stonework, much of it prefabricated, was transported all the way from Lisbon (304km/188mi). The town is laid out in rectangular plan around the black-and-white-paved square, which bears Pombal's name and has an obelisk to the memory of the then reigning monarch José. It stands at the mouth of the River Guadiana, facing the Spanish town of Ayamonte, to which there is a regular ferry service for passengers and cars. There is little to be seen apart from a small museum of printing.

Most of the tunny caught along the coast is brought here for canning and the town is in fact known as the 'tunny exchange'. From its port also is shipped copper ore from the local mine of São Domingos, an extension of the more famous deposits of Rio Tinto in Spain. The attractive holiday resort of **Monte**

*Santa Maria do Castelo, Tavira.*

**Gordo** with miles of sandy beach is 4km/2.5mi west. North (2km/1.25mi) is **Castro Marim** (pop. 5000), headquarters of the Knights of Christ before they moved to Tomar in 1334. Their castle, 14th-century but part 12th-century, is open to the public. On nearby hills can be seen the Church of Our Lady of Martyrs (*Nossa Senhora dos Mártires*) and the fort of *São Sebastião*, built by João IV (1640–56), father of Henry II's wife, Catharine of Bragança. *Faro 52km/32mi.*

*East of Silves, near Alte, home of the golden fleece?*

# INDEX

All main entries are printed in heavy type. Map references are also printed in heavy type.
The map page number precedes the grid reference.